The Search for Identity

The Search for Identity

Disciples of Christ—
The Restructure Years (1960-1985)

Robert L. Friedly and

D. Duane Cummins

A community is involved in retelling its story, its constitutive narrative, and in so doing, it offers examples of the men and women who have embodied and exemplified the meaning of the community. These stories of collective history and exemplary individuals are an important part of the tradition that is so central to a community of memory.
—Robert Bellah and associates, *Habits of the Heart.*

CBP Press
St. Louis, Missouri

Unless otherwise indicated, all scripture quotations are from the Revised Standard Version of the Bible, copyrighted 1946, 1952, © 1971, 1973, by the Division of Christian Education of the National Council of Churches of Christ in the United States of America.

Library of Congress Cataloging-in-Publication Data

Friedly, Robert L.
    The search for identity : Disciples of Christ—the restructure years / Robert L. Friedly and D. Duane Cummins.

    ISBN 0-8272-3427-9
    1. Christian Church (Disciples of Christ)—History—20th century.
2. Christian Church (Disciples of Christ—Government.
I. Cummins, D. Duane.   II. Title.
BX7316.F74 1987   1987
286.6—dc19   87-21916

Printed in the United States of America

Contents

Preface

This is a contemporary history of the Disciples of Christ. It is intended to be *authoritative* but not scholarly, *encompassing* but not a slavish documentation, *reflective* but not overly analytical, concerned with the *important* but equally concerned with the *interesting*.

In short, it is a book written by two lay persons for Disciples grass roots church readers. As such, it concentrates on people, not program. Where material had to be cut, the attempt was made to save the anecdotes at the expense of the bureaucratic. Some leaders and events have been omitted that probably should have been included. But our first concern was a readable history, a popular treatment, a "feel" for the Disciples of Christ and their contemporary struggle for an identity.

We have divided each chapter into three segments. The opening segment of each chapter (except the first) contains a listing of events and dates for given years, placing the benchmarks of the Disciples Search for Identity in the historic context. The events cited for each year are important milestones along the way.

The second segment of each chapter is history narrative. It basically follows the chronology of the last quarter century but darts into the past for foundation stones and into the future for finishing trim.

The third section of each chapter describes the singular Witness of an individual—not necessarily the most significant persons of the period but certainly among the most fascinating. While the institution rumbles along, a million Disciples are witnessing daily in their lives. It is to those one million Disciples that we address this book.

—The Authors

7

1

Rejoicing in A New Identity

Orange and white decorative circles the size of barrel tops ringed the balcony railing at 15-foot intervals in the oval-shaped Kansas City Municipal Auditorium that Saturday afternoon, September 28, 1968. On each of the white circles identical, stylized, orange lettering proclaimed: "We Rejoice in God." The phrase had been lifted from a remarkable document that was about to become the central expression of a million Christians who for the first time in their century and a half of existence would be a denomination and able to call themselves a "church." Up until that time they had been a "brotherhood," a word they used to avoid being thought of as a denomination, because denominations were human-made divisions in the one body of Christ and therefore an evil. In the dim light near the roof opposite the makeshift stage a huge clock, its face lighted, displayed 3:35. For the annual convention-goers of the Disciples of Christ, six years of struggle, soul-searching, intensity—and what some thought to be diversion from mission—were about to end. For these Disciples and their forbears the frustration of 119 years of trying to carry the gospel to the world without an adequate vehicle showed promise of ending as well.

The soft-spoken, sandy-haired professor looked out at that great congregation of eight thousand before him and in the glaring lights of the stage blinked at the prepared script on the lectern. Without any vocal trace of recognition of the magnitude of the moment he intoned: "Are you ready to vote?—you are—all those in favor of Resolution Number 55, please stand." Applause began immediately and a soft "woooo" and a couple of whistles rose from the gathering as a great wave brought thousands to their feet. Allowing but 12 seconds for that celebration, the presider interrupted, "Thank you, we're still taking a vote, so be seated. Will those opposed to the motion please stand." A smattering of people rose. More applause. "Thank you for your vote and for being here to register it. The chair declares that the motion has carried by the necessary two-thirds vote and the Provisional Design as amended is adopted."

A great smile spread across the face of the presiding officer, Ronald E. Osborn, 51-years-old and dean of Christian Theological Seminary in Indianapolis. He felt elation, gratitude, relief—a momentous decision having been made. Jean Woolfolk, a Little Rock insurance executive who in five years would become the first woman moderator, saw tears gather in the corners of Osborn's eyes. Four years earlier in Louisville, Kentucky, Osborn had captured superbly in three lectures the mind of the church's Commission on Brotherhood Restructure and where the commission wanted to go with this historic organizing of a people. It was one of those key moments that led to this new moment which Osborn now savored.

Earlier in this session and the one before lunch, twelve final amendments to *A Provisional Design for the Christian Church (Disciples of Christ)* had been laboriously considered, five of them being approved and seven rejected. They dealt with such things as adding another "voluntarily" to the text where reference was made to how congregations related to the structure. The formal adoption vote was a sure thing. The previous year's convention in St. Louis had recommended it. After that, the required two-thirds of the state organizations and two-thirds of the general agencies had voted to participate.

Most Disciples had been on the periphery of the process no matter how hard leaders tried to involve them; they had listened to talk of restructure for nearly a decade. To them, this was the vote that counted. When Osborn calmly announced the result the body rose to its feet in a wave. There was a thunder of applause mixed with muffled voices, lasting 30 seconds, and then the singing of the Doxology. The singing wasn't spontaneous as everybody remembers; it was in their mythologizing of that moment. In fact, Osborn asked song leader Bill Guthrie to lead it. "Praise God from whom all blessings flow . . ." Here was a people truly rejoicing in God.

Kenneth L. Teegarden, one of the shaping architects of the new structure, drew to his feet from a chair at the rear of the platform and joined in the singing. As administrative secretary of restructure, he was close at hand to answer inquiries. His knowledge of the structure document was photo-copy perfect. Often, without intending to, he had overwhelmed local gatherings of Disciples to whom he spoke, drying up questions with intimidating knowledge. Physically pencil-thin, his energy throughout the process had been inexhaustible. Later he was to joke when named the second general minister and president of the church that he was "Exhibit A" in the Disciples' determination to have a "lean general office."

Granville T. Walker and W. A. Welsh had come into the process while pastors in Texas of two of the Disciples' largest congregations, 30 miles apart in Fort Worth and Dallas. Walker chaired the restructure commission, Welsh its "nature, design and authority" task force. Each had been president of the International Convention for one year. With the vote now recorded, Welsh mumbled in relief: "We're through." They weren't, of course. The job of putting flesh on the new structure was still ahead and Welsh, the younger of the two, would be a member of the committee assigned that task and would later become a member of the church's General Cabinet. Walker had been offered the opportunity of a seconding speech when business item No. 55 had been introduced a short while earlier. To applause, Walker echoed the words on the auditorium railing: "Rejoicing in God, I second this motion," a brevity that caused Osborn to remark to the whole convention, with a chuckle, that surely it was the shortest speech the pastor ever made and probably the best.

A. Dale Fiers and Gertrude Dimke were seated side by side at a table on the platform. She had been secretary of the convention for 22 years and was destined to remain another decade in the new General Assembly office. Her presence was a symbol of the gathered church at the national/international level as she fronted every session of assembly and board. He was the father-figure executive of the convention who had come to the position from a dozen years as head of the church's principal international mission agency, the United Christian Missionary Society. He epitomized the upright, moral Christian leader.

It was difficult—impossible—for those who grew up in awe of his name to call him "Dale." That included Teegarden, who at 46 was fourteen years younger than Fiers. Dr. Fiers shortly would become the first General Minister and President. Perhaps more than any other, the vision of "church" as opposed to some configuration of churches (congregations) in the plural, was his. Osborn once had suggested "Communion of Christian Churches" as the concept. Fiers would not be moved. A restructure commission subcommittee early had called for a "general association of Christian Churches." But the visionaries were not about to settle for something less than a full understanding of church. Fiers maintained that, since Disciples believed baptism is into the whole church rather than into a single congregation, the baptismal act conveyed membership in the regional expression of the church and in the national/international (general) church as well. One gathering was church just as surely as the other. Whether two or three gathered in the name of Jesus—or two or three thousand— there was the Christ in the midst. And it was the church.

Undoubtedly many in the 1968 assembly were asking themselves following the vote: "What do we do next?" But "next" had been thought out carefully. Tuesday the International Convention of Christian Churches (Disciples of Christ) would be adjourned "sine die," or without a date fixed for meeting again. It would never reconvene. Then Tuesday evening, October 1, the General Assembly of the Christian Church (Disciples of Christ) would be gaveled into session by Osborn, who would be both the last president of what had been and first moderator of what now was. The "provisional" General Assembly would continue for one additional day. The General Assembly would convene in full session the next year, 1969, in Seattle and then every two years after that.

The fact that the restructure plan had been conceived, weighed, drafted, and accepted only six years from the constituting of the Commission on Brotherhood Restructure was testimony to the urgency Disciples felt for re-ordering their procedures. George G. Beazley Jr., the ecumenical officer whose experience was with interdenominational structure, had predicted it would take 20 years. Convention executive Fiers, always optimistic but generally cautious, had maintained it could be done within the decade of the 1960s.

The September 28, 1968, vote was the most significant action organizationally for Disciples of Christ in 136 years. Frontiersman Andrew Jackson was President of the United States when, first in Georgetown, Kentucky, and then in Lexington as 1831 ended and 1832 began, Alexander Campbell's Disciples shook hands with Barton W. Stone's Christians and the two frontier religious movements became one. The 1968 dropping of the letters "e" and "s" from "churches" may have had a cosmetic appearance to it—but there was no small issue at stake. For a body that had denied its existence as a denomination all those years because of its heritage of protest against the sinful denominational divisions in the church, it was a major philosophical and theological step, taken in the interest of trying to maintain a semblance of a structured mission beyond the congregation.

The roughly 4,000 congregations and one million persons representing the core of the cooperating Disciples of Christ in the United States and Canada in 1968 had made a statement. They needed each other for mission. They would no longer be the euphemistic "brotherhood"—no longer a convention of individuals from local churches, but a church. They would claim each other even though it meant the loss of fellow Christians who could be wooed away by radical congregationalists who trusted no structure beyond the local and who felt mission in company with non-Disciples was unacceptable compromise. No longer would Disciples ministries in national and world settings be undertaken by church "agencies" that by-and-large owed allegiance to separate, self-perpetuating boards comprised of focused-interest individuals. Disciples had identified themselves openly as a "church"—not the whole church, as that would have been antithetical to their heritage—but as a church that manifested itself beyond the congregations in "regions" and in "general administrative units"—units to be called divisions and councils of the church and responsible to a delegate assembly.

The word "general" always would be used instead of "national" because two nations, not one, comprised the Christian Church (Disciples of Christ). Though Canadians represented less than one half of one percent of Disciples' North America membership and organizationally were but one of 39 regions in the new structure, their contribution to the church over the years was singular and their spokespersons powerful. A Canadian, Archibald McLean, had shaped and molded unified overseas mission work among the Disciples in the first part of the twentieth century. Jessie Trout founded the Christian Women's Fellowship, one of the most influential groups in the church. Other active Canadians constantly reminded Disciples of the two-nation character of their church.

The newly-adopted structure was unique in Christendom. It

13

drew its character from a gathering that was a hybrid of mass meeting and representative democracy. Everyone who registered for the new every-odd-year General Assembly could debate and otherwise participate except vote. The vote was representative. Each congregation and each region that wanted to be represented could be. There were no legal bonds, despite the charges of "connectionalism" spread by opponents of the concept. There was no pyramid of authority. For that reason, leaders avoided use of the word "levels" in describing the congregational, regional, general structure arrangement. They adopted—essentially by default, since no one could think of a better word—the cumbersome term "manifestations" instead.

Congregation and region and general unit each would be responsible for its own property, its own financial affairs and its own ministry. The sole bond was a biblical-style covenant through which church issues were decided by mutual agreement. Human beings being human, it would not always work, and major questions of authority were left unanswered. Funding, without forced apportionments, remained tenuous, both in collection and distribution. Those who claimed that a new power unleashed by the changed structure would take over the property of congregations were proved wrong. Some of those who hoped that restructure would produce radically-servant Christianity were disappointed. Overall, the new structure worked well enough that Disciples dropped the term "provisional" from their design document nine years later, satisfied that they had no need of a constitution. They would live under the *Design*.

The quarter century, 1960-85, neatly encompasses what many call the Restructure Years in the history of the Christian Church (Disciples of Christ). The year 1960 marks the approval in convention of a restructure commission, and 1985 dates the retirement of the last of the central restructure figures. In between there was the process of conceiving, conceptualizing, promoting, enacting, embracing and shaping a church organization. But to think that restructure was the history of those years fails to grasp the full story. Historical accuracy calls for a more comprehensive look. Those years encompassed an intensive Search for Identity. There were four powerful developments during the period, in addition to restructure, that both propelled and impeded that search.

1. The Decline of Membership

One of the general social phenomena of the mid-1960s was the start of a long decline in membership for North American mainline Protestant churches. Some analysts attributed the decline to the gradual winnowing of what was believed to have been an artificial "growth" in the 1950s. A British research organization, Oxford Analytica, wrote in 1986 that 1950s church growth in America was a "public celebration" of post World War II American success rather than "intense personal experience."

The more conservative Christians in the activist 1960s blamed the loss of members on social action, claiming that Christians were deserting because the church stopped preaching the gospel and began "secular humanist" political and social pursuits. The view that membership losses resulted from dissatisfaction over social involvements was dealt a severe blow in 1972. In that year the North American Interchurch Study—the most extensive study ever undertaken among North American churches—showed that Christians wanted their denominations to speak out on social issues and to support ethnic minority groups. Not only were people not leaving the church over social issues but 94 percent said they never had withheld contributions due to a church social stance. The 1972 study quoted one churchman: "My own faith has moved out of the church and into the secular world. I feel I teach Sunday school all the time in work." Society simply offered too many non-church opportunities for satisfying personal growth and service needs. The increasing age of the average church member in the 1980s lent credence to the belief that the mainline Protestant church wasn't challenging young people either. Fully 62 percent of Disciples of Christ in the mid-1980s were 55 years old or older. Yet 40 percent of U.S. adults were in the 18-34 age range.

Further, those things that marked the growing evangelical churches—passionate personal experiences, strong authority, and narrow definitions of identity—were diametrically opposite Disciples concepts of rational faith, mutuality in decisions, and respect for diversity. Reason, democracy and openness were accompanied to some degree by a "live and let live" attitude that weakened evangelism efforts of the church.

For Disciples the membership decline began in 1965. Growth was a "given" through the church's first 133 years. But in 1965

15

there was a drop of 1,981 members and the following year fully one percent of the membership was lost. The Sunday church school provided the early warning with the beginning of its decline as far back as 1958. With the exception of the period of withdrawal of the nominally-related "independent" churches over restructure in the late 1960s, the membership losses continued at about one to three percent per year, the smaller amounts dominating the 1980s and offering hope of a reversal. The losses served as a rallying cry for those dissatisfied with church leadership, leaving Disciples leaders defensive about the decline and in need of a new sense of, and means to, evangelism.

The major withdrawal of congregations from the church *Year Book and Directory* near the time of the restructure vote officially ended the long and painful relationship between Disciples and congregations called "Independents." Many Independent congregations were unaware they were listed with the Disciples. Agitation by restructure opponents changed that. Sometimes there were struggles for the minds and hearts of congregations between Disciples and Independents when local churches changed pastors and, often unwittingly, called Independent-leaning ministers. There was bitterness when church buildings, constructed with funds raised by cooperative Disciples, became the meeting places of Independents who saw no need of helping other cooperatives.

The unwillingness of Disciples to exclude anyone was a reason the break had not occurred earlier. How could a non-doctrinal, non-dogmatic melting pot for all Christians practice exclusion? In addition, there was a natural pride in numbers of adherents. The Independents, with their own institutions since 1927, formalized the separation. It can be said that an end came to troublesome family infighting and recrimination when the Independents, absent from home for more than four decades, finally changed their address. Editor-historian Howard E. Short suggests that is precisely what happened. Relationships in 1986 were much more relaxed between Disciples and Independents than in 1960, he says. Disciples finally were content to let the Independents go their own way, thereby divesting any vision among Disciples of trying to restore some idealized first century church. "Restoration" of the New Testament church in all its simplicity and purity was one of the twin foci of the Christian Churches (Disciples of Christ) in its origins on the American frontier. The other was

Christian unity. The more conservative elements of the movement took the Restoration road, the Disciples the unity path.

The Independents who finally took their names out of the *Year Book* represented some 3,500 congregations and three quarters of a million members, which would have been devastating had not the relationship been so limited and the support of Disciples outreach so small. Between 1967 and 1968 alone, 2,106 congregations removed their names from the *Year Book* (26 percent of the total congregations in the book). But during the same period dollar support of Disciples world causes actually grew by two percent.

2. The ecumenism explosion

Another of the forces strongly influencing the search for identity was the virtual explosion of ecumenical activity at the outset of the 1960s. Though the organic church union aspects of the ecumenical flurry subsided somewhat in the 1970s and 1980s, the overall fervor rekindled historic Disciples' concerns for unity and both stimulated and challenged their self-image as the standard-bearers of Christian unity. The Disciples throughout their existence—and indeed as the reason for their existence—professed an abiding passion for the unity of all Christendom. During the quarter century 1960-1985 exciting ecumenical developments gave Disciples an opportunity for leadership in the field but also tested the seriousness of their commitment.

Simply put, the Christian unity heritage of the Christian Church (Disciples of Christ) was this: Both of the early wings of the movement—the Disciples in western Pennsylvania and the Christians in eastern Kentucky—felt denominational division was a sin that hampered the church witness in the world. If Christians would adhere to a simple biblical faith and would tolerate each other's opinions love would prevail. Unity, therefore, was the "polar star" which guided their journey in faith.

In response to that unity passion, Disciples were at the forefront of everything ecumenical. They helped organize the World Council of Churches in 1948 and the National Council of Churches of Christ in the U.S.A. two years later. The World Council was the setting in the mid-1980s for the development of a remarkable theological convergence. The convergence on baptism, the Lord's Supper and the ministry would serve as the basis for future union and unity configurations.

Single-project, single-issue and single-approach cooperative or "consortia" arrangements between denominations also generally involved Disciples. One of the most significant of these was Joint Educational Development, which brought together fourteen denominations in one configuration or another in the development of Christian education resources. The period saw the dawn of the Consultation on Church Union, which represented the churches of 25 million Americans, including the Disciples. While a Plan of Union proposed by COCU in 1970 hit a stone wall, the principles behind it became the basis for experimental life together as an approach to union in place of legislated arrangements. COCU also secured promises by the churches (including the Disciples in 1975) to work toward removing obstacles to "mutual recognition of members."

The United Church of Christ, a union of four denominations, one of them out of the same Barton W. Stone background as Disciples, emerged as the principal two-way unity dialogue partner for the Disciples of Christ. In 1985 that dialogue expanded into an "ecumenical partnership" that promised joint work in mission, in worship, in theological study, and efforts toward mutual recognition of members and ministers, perhaps someday to eventuate in deeper links, including "common decision-making."

Canadian Disciples found themselves in a three-way union conversation with the United Church of Canada and the Anglicans, a series of talks that ended unsuccessfully. Vatican II, at the outset of the period, made an ecumenical hero of Pope John XXIII and planted a huge new partner on the ecumenical scene. The Roman Catholic Church, in the Disciples' early days, had been a symbol to the frontier Christians of abusive power and restrictive theology, but now it became a one-to-one theological dialogue partner with Disciples.

Similar bilateral talks with the Russian Orthodox Church began in 1987. Disciples happily initiated or responded in connection with all these ecumenical overtures but often found their own membership unaware of the church's unity heritage or found some of them almost uncompromisingly rigid in practices and attitudes that belied the heritage. Research showed that about half of the church members had their church origins in other denominations.

3. The Liberation of "Missions"

Perhaps the most traumatic change influencing the identity search was the coming of age of churches in the third world and the decolonization of the mission fields. Africa exploded with two dozen new nations at the outset of the 1960s. People who could lead nations believed they could lead churches as well. The image of the Bible-carrying missionary preaching the gospel to half-clothed natives in a jungle was a caricature to be sure. Nevertheless, there remained powerful visions in the pews that North Americans preaching to less fortunates abroad constituted "foreign" missions.

The idea of partner churches in mission was slow to spread, perhaps because of the decline in Sunday schools and church schools as vehicles to convey it. Perhaps it also was difficult for North Americans to visualize themselves as the recipients of missionary concern from abroad, a necessity in any legitimate two-way arrangement. But new nations and new churches were born in the former mission fields. The young third world churches were freed from missionary management. Missionary numbers were reduced extensively.

With the changes came fewer personal rewards for North Americans. The more paternalistic approach to mission made it easier for Western Christians to see their good work and identify with it. De-emphasis on the missionaries (now called "overseas staff" because of the negatives borne by the term missionary), more emphasis on the host church as the decision-maker and manager of the mission, and more ecumenical sharing contributed to the identity crisis of Disciples concerning their overseas ministry. The poor and the oppressed, identified by Jesus as his focus of mission, would become a central concern. But that all meant more difficulty in pinpointing specifically what mission dollars were going to what project, subverting the giver's desire to experience the joy of seeing the direct result. It meant more controversy because dealing with the poor and the oppressed created social, economic and political resistance, just as it did in Jesus' day.

North America's political involvements with other countries

around the world added to the complexities. Church members' allegiance to their country and allegiance to Christian principles sometimes were confused and in conflict. The U.S. government provided support to friendly right-wing dictators in many countries where Disciples were helping the poor and oppressed gain economic independence which, in turn, became threatening to repressive governments. Overseas Christians often expressed their involvement in the struggle in terms of "liberation theology." That brought condemnation from some North American Christians who saw it as Christian participation in or encouragement of violent overthrow of governments and cozying up to Communism. It brought a new sense of mission to other Christians who saw it in the context of God's liberation of the Hebrews from Egypt and Jesus' liberation of poor, oppressed, blind, infirm from the principalities and powers of the world that stood between them and more abundant life.

4. The Struggle for Justice

Finally, the church's involvement in the struggle for justice that grew out of the 1960s civil rights movement and continued through various liberation and dignity struggles provided a new set of questions about identity. At the very moment Disciples began to redefine their "movement" as an institution, along came the social movements of the 1960s—secular as well as religious—movements seeking justice, liberation, civil rights, peace—biblical concerns but powerfully threatening to institutions, including the institution of the church. These movements would pit Disciples against each other over the social, economic and political implications, if not theological. What did love of neighbor really mean? The searching years would see the rise of people's movements and force Disciples to deal with them.

Since the concept of justice is so biblically firm, the church could not avoid identifying with it during these volatile decades. That identification was not without pain as justice claims often ran counter to basic patriotic instincts. A priority for peace identified in 1981 would not be spoken of without the added concept of justice. How was peace with justice to be translated in connection with the Vietnam War? How was it translated in dealing with young people who went to war to protect their country's freedoms and those who refused to go due to their Christian objection to the killing? How was justice to be applied in making up for more than two centuries of wrongs to blacks in the United States? Where was the justice in responding to the commitment of women to the ministry when roadblocks remained in education and many pulpits were closed to any but men? What was justice in relation to the poor, the oppressed, and the outcasts?

A Cultural Context for the Search

It is ironic that the Disciples of Christ began structuring their faith institution just as an extreme anti-institutional attitude arrived on the North American scene. John Naisbitt in *Megatrends* wrote that individuals lost confidence in structures and "began to disengage from the institutions that had disillusioned them and to relearn the ability to take action on their own." Robert Bellah and associates in a recent sociological study of America, *Habits of the Heart*, observed that what "failed at every level, from the society of nations to the national society to the local community to the family is integration: we have failed to remember our community as members of the same body." While Disciples tried to build a representative and workable structure, the society around the church was fragmenting.

Even in a more settled time, the church—as it tries to build community—contends with the individualism that is so much a part of the American ethos. The cult of individualism plays havoc with the effort to define authority in a structure, the need to educate to the wider world mission, the role of promoting Christian unity and the identification with the poor and oppressed. Robert Bellah observes: "When thinking of the imperative to 'love thy neighbor,' many metropolitan Americans . . . consider that responsibility fulfilled when they love those compatible neighbors they have surrounded themselves with, fellow members of their own lifestyle enclave, while letting the rest of the world go its chaotic, mysterious way."

Again, Bellah, in *Habits of the Heart*, maintains that Americans are unable to piece together a picture of the whole society and how they fit into it. "The claims of large groups of people are simply seen as competing wants, not as matters of justice and therefore are interpreted in terms of power." If that is true, it would help explain the resistance among some church people to social justice and liberation involvements. Those efforts would be seen simply as power plays, not matters of justice.

English philosopher John Locke, from whom early Disciples leaders were said to have drawn their emphasis on a rational faith, was a spokesperson for individualism. Bellah describes Locke's position: "The individual is prior to society, which comes into existence only through the voluntary contract of individuals trying to maximize their own self-interest." Further, said Bellah and his *Habits* colleagues: "Individualism lies at the very core of American culture. . . . Anything that would violate our right to think for ourselves, judge for ourselves, make our own decisions, live our lives as we see fit, is not only morally wrong, it is sacrilegious." That is the stuff of which opposition to a new structure is made.

Historian Arthur Schlesinger Jr. reminds us, too, of the role that civil religion plays in shaping or hindering the church in its attempt to make a witness on social issues. Schlesinger wrote in his 1986 *Cycles of American History* that all nations succumb to the fantasy of innate superiority. Americans, he said, have believed from the country's beginnings that somehow the United States is the special province of God. "The fact that God had withheld America so long—until the Reformation purified the church, until the invention of printing spread Scripture among the people—argued that he had been saving the new land for some ultimate manifestation of his grace. . . . The new land was certainly a part, perhaps the climax, of redemptive history; America was divine prophecy fulfilled. The covenant of salvation, it seemed, had passed from the Jews to the American colonists." Born on the American frontier and steeped in the ideal of the American revolution, Disciples have had to contend with their own dose of civil religion.

It Happened in 1960

Four events of 1960 were pivotal moments that bear mentioning. On January 9 a committee of the Disciples International Convention meeting at McCormick's Creek, Indiana, voted to recommend the appointment of a restructure commission to propose some orderly solution to the chaos of agencies, societies, individuals and congregations that represented the Disciples of Christ. Three weeks later, on the first of February, four black students in Greensboro, North Carolina, sat down at a white-only lunch counter in Woolworth's and refused to budge, inaugurating the sit-ins that would be a major element of the civil rights struggle. On June 30, the Belgian Congo, the territory encompassing the largest of the Disciples overseas mission involvements, received its independence and soon would join the exploding family of African nations as Zaire. On December 4, just prior to the opening of the National Council of Churches assembly in San Francisco, Presbyterian Eugene Carson Blake mounted the pulpit of Grace Episcopal Cathedral in that city with a captivating unity proposal. It resulted in the nine-denomination Consultation on Church Union.

Each of these events triggered a strong response among Disciples. But it may have been an occurrence in the Soviet Union on May 1 that altered the context within which the Disciples' identity search for the next twenty-five years would take place. On May 1, as Disciples were drafting a resolution to create the Commission on Brotherhood Restructure, a young pilot named Francis Gary Powers (a member of an Independent Christian Church and a Milligan College alumnus), working secretly for the U.S. Central Intelligence Agency and taking pictures five miles above Central Russia, was shot down by Soviet gunners.

President Eisenhower first denied the overflight, having been assured that the Russians could not have downed the supersecret U-2 aircraft and that neither pilot nor craft could have survived if they had. Then when the Russians put the very-much-alive Powers on display and publicly showed the camera equipment and even a spy-novel-style suicide needle, the U.S. admitted the mission.

It was a loss of innocence for many Americans—an innocence that would be difficult to comprehend in the 1980s following two decades of Bay of Pigs, Gulf of Tonkin, Watergate, My Lai, Chile, the Contras and Iran. World War II had baptized American virtue; it was clear there was a good side and a bad side, and it was only the enemy that spied and lied. That idealism had remained during the 1950s growth and prosperity period. To discover suddenly the disillusioning truth was to put at risk the confidence in government—the largest of American institutions.

As icon after icon tumbled in the flurry of assassinations, covert operations, surveillance, police brutality, race and political violence and war news that followed in the 1960s, every institution—not just government—came to be suspect. The Francis Gary Powers incident may have triggered the general anti-institutionalism just at the moment the Disciples had chosen finally to identify and shape their institution. For Disciples the loss of innocence represented the rewriting of the rules just as the game began.

* * *

"Stories of . . . exemplary individuals are an important part of the tradition that is so central to a community of memory."

In that late fall of 1960 a tall, dour Disciples of Christ industrialist stood before the applauding assemblage of church people in San Francisco and accepted his election for three years as the president of the National Council of Churches. He was the first layperson to be so honored. But J. IRWIN MILLER was no average layperson. How many of the laity read their New Testaments in the original Greek? How many hire ethicists to advise their companies on the morality of company actions and proposals? How many challenge fellow business people to redefine competition in terms of love of neighbor? How many maintain regular church attendance, serve as elder and teach church school while jetting around the world to manage eighteen plants on four continents, employing 14,000 people and selling two billion dollars worth of diesel engines each year?

Miller, chairman of Cummins Engine, in the small town of Columbus, Indiana, 35 miles south of Indianapolis, was the man of the hour for the church council. He was to lead the council during its early involvements with the civil rights movement. While he was president, the National Council of Churches helped organize the March on Washington, which culminated in Martin Luther King Jr.'s "I Have a Dream" speech. Three years after the King speech Miller moderated a panel at the Disciples assembly in Dallas which featured Dr. King as a speaker. Miller raised a question with a dissenter on the panel: How can civil disobedience by blacks obeying their consciences be opposed by a nation that after World War II hanged Nazis for obeying superiors and failing to apply their consciences? *Esquire* magazine later profiled Miller's face life-size on its cover and wrote a major article about him headed: "Is it too late for a man of honesty, high purpose and intelligence to be elected President of the United States in 1968?"

Joseph Irwin Miller was born May 26, 1909. Both grandfathers had been Disciples preachers. One of them, Z. T. Sweeney, was president of the church's general convention in 1904. Miller's family had been involved in Indiana politics and had earned money in dry goods, banking, supermarkets, tinplate and starch. After graduating from Yale in 1931 and Oxford (Master of Arts) in 1933, Miller was given the general managership of a business making diesel engines that weren't selling well to truck manufacturers. There were sixty employees in 1934 at the Cummins Engine Company. But Clessie Cummins, a family friend, preferred experimenting with fuel pumps and injector systems to managing the business. So Miller had taken over management and in thirty years, with two years off for World War II Navy service, had built the diesel business into one of the largest in the world.

Miller won many awards and honors, but one in particular gave him a chance to counsel his colleagues in the higher echelons of American business. In 1978 he received the top award of Religion in American Life for business people who practice their faith. At the award dinner in New York City's Waldorf-Astoria, March 14, Miller told dozens of the chief executives of America's biggest corporations—many of whom had strong reservations about activist churches: "The business of religion is not to support the status quo. Its business is to speak, uncomfortably if necessary, until it is heard. Those of us, like myself, who are in business and want to survive in business, need this practical advice for survival, unpalatable though we usually find it."

When the World Council of Churches was under one of the periodic attacks from media in 1971, the council turned to someone with classic American capitalist credentials for help in dealing with charges of anti-American and anti-capitalist actions by the council. Miller was happy to respond. *Reader's Digest* had carried two articles in the fall of 1971 criticizing the World Council for its social involvements, tying those involvements to objectives of international Communism. Angry church people deluged the Council and member denomination offices with calls and mail, wondering if the charges were true. Top World Council officials in the United States and other American church leaders were just as angry, knowing the charges to be false.

One morning in New York's 475 Riverside Drive, church leaders met with the two top editors of *Reader's Digest* to appeal for redress. They demanded two articles to answer the charges. The magazine agreed to a single article, specifying that the article could state the World Council's position but could not refute the charges made in the earlier writings. Further, the *Digest* would have to agree on the person chosen as author. The Disciples communication officer, one of those present, suggested Miller. The *Digest* editors promptly agreed.

Miller consented to do the article for the April 1972 issue of the *Digest* and accepted the constraints of not being permitted to answer the specific charges. In Miller's article, he laid out a classic rationale for the church's social involvements. "Many of us, without too much thought," he wrote, "equate religion with joining a church, attending worship there, giving to its budget and behaving reasonably well in our private lives. But Jesus waged all-out war on the limitations of just such a concept. Listen to him upbraiding the scribes and Pharisees: 'You tithe . . . but you have neglected the weightier matters of the law—justice, mercy, faith.' In his description of the Last Judgment, Jesus says that the determination of the righteous is to be made, not on the basis of church membership and theological correctness, but on the way people behave, on their 'social actions.'"

Miller told the millions of *Digest* readers that the church is inescapably involved in sensitive, difficult, and controversial social action. There is no way, he said, that the World Council of Churches, or even local congregations, can play it safe and be true to the gospel. Nor can the church confine its preaching to individuals. "This is an age of organizations—business, labor, universities, government. A serious question is now before us: Is any group of human beings organized for a particular purpose exempt from those laws of human behavior and accepted morality which are considered binding on each member as an individual?" Out of its concern for human beings, said Miller, the church must speak to them about their individual and corporate behavior with both words and deeds. "Whose job is it to cause society to 'repent,' if not the church's? The church dare not evade its obligation to proclaim God's judgment over all human activity, even as it proclaims his mercy and forgiveness."

Reader's Digest sent Miller $1,000 for the article, which the writer forwarded to the World Council of Churches with the comment: "Please accept this as probably the only contribution you'll ever get from the *Reader's Digest!*"

2

How the Search Began

1961—*U.S., Cuba break relations* (Jan. 3) . . . *J. F. Kennedy inaugurated President* (Jan. 20) . . . Restructure commission office established (February) . . . *USSR's Gagarin first man in space* (April 12) . . . *Bay of Pigs invasion fails* (April 17) . . . *Shepard in sub-orbital flight* (May 5) . . . Second CWF Quadrennial held (July 19-23) . . . *Berlin wall erected* (Aug. 13) . . . Kansas City convention urges support of UN, disarmament (Sept. 29—Oct. 4) . . . *USSR tests 50-megaton bomb* (Oct. 29).

1962—First talks held with United Church of Christ (Feb. 19-21) . . . *Glenn first American in orbit* (Feb. 20) . . . COCU organized in Washington (April) . . . *Algeria gains sovereignty* (July 3) . . . Los Angeles convention okays 126 on restructure commission (Sept. 30-Oct. 4) . . . *First Black enters U. of Mississippi* (Oct. 1) . . . *Pope John XXIII convenes Vatican II* (Oct. 11) . . . *Cuba missile crisis* (Oct. 22) . . . First meeting of restructure commission (Oct. 30-Nov. 1) . . . *Rachel Carson triggers environmental movement with* Silent Spring.

He had a Churchillian look about him: squat, gruff, stubborn, confident. His wit was dry. Associates described him as a master organizer. Blunt and talented were other descriptions. Some believed him to be a manipulator. He had a way of getting things done. Willard M. Wickizer is given much of the credit by his colleagues as having sparked the restructure process among the Disciples of Christ. A Maryville, Missouri, pastor until he joined the United Christian Missionary Society staff April 15, 1936, he first served the UCMS as director of church development and evangelism. By the time of the beginnings of the restructure era he was executive chairman of the UCMS Division of Home Missions. In that role he was responsible for much of the national/international church relationship with states and congregations.

Wickizer's organizational mind was appalled by the disarray of Disciples' structures. There was little coordination of resources, schedules and facilities on behalf of efficiency and church wholeness. He decided to do something to correct it. As early as 1936 he spoke to the state secretaries about the need to coordinate program. Soon after World War II some of the states would begin to bring the women's work, men's work, social action, Christian education and missionary societies in the state under their collective wing.

Wickizer served as the staff executive for the Home and State Missions Planning Council, formed by the Denver International Convention in 1938. Home and State, which met biennially, brought together local church leaders, state leaders and national leaders for several days of strategizing the church's program at all levels in the areas of local church life, evangelism, effective ministry, town and country church, Christian service, missionary policy and strategy, world outreach, urban work and stewardship. Most of those areas related directly to the Home Missions division for which Wickizer was responsible. In 1950 he was involved in the establishment of the National Church Program Coordinating Council set up to coordinate the development of program materials in the Christian education, higher education, women's and stewardship fields.

The Panel of Scholars

In 1956, Wickizer and Harlie L. Smith, president of the Board of Higher Education of the church, convinced their directors to underwrite jointly a "panel of scholars"—unprecedented in a church that had a history of nervousness about elitism—to define the theological underpinnings of mid-twentieth century Disciples. Where exactly did Disciples stand on theological matters? Where were they going? What were their theological issues? Since these considerations had much to do with the Disciples understanding of the nature of the church, they had much to say about the structure for doing business.

Wickizer explained that Disciples' founders were profound scholars and practical theologians. Yet, in recent years, Disciples had become so caught up in practical church operations they had not been too greatly concerned about theology. "Many of the convictions originally held by our founding fathers are being challenged today and on every hand the question is being raised, 'Just what do Disciples of Christ believe?'" The Panel of Scholars—three local pastors and fourteen theologians from nine different colleges and seminaries—were to help Disciples of Christ reexamine their beliefs and doctrines in a scholarly way. The idea was to "stimulate additional scholarly thought," in Wickizer's words.

The scholars convened twice a year beginning in 1957 and by 1962, the year of the formation of the Commission on Brotherhood Restructure, they had produced forty essays evaluating Disciples thought. It was a monumental effort, chaired first by Howard E. Short, professor of church history at the College of the Bible (now Lexington Theological Seminary) in Kentucky, and then by W. Barnett Blakemore, dean of Disciples Divinity House, University of Chicago. Among the observations of scholars on the panel: The attempt to restore the New Testament Church in the twentieth century (Restorationism) had no validity for the Disciples of Christ, whatever its historical link to the movement. The autonomy of the congregation was a recent concept and should be tempered with equal autonomy in various levels of church life. The Disciples in fact represented a separate denomination and ought to acknowledge it rather than try to wish it away. Disciples' congregationalism reflected their frontier origins and not the New Testament.

Those thoughts certainly were grist for the restructure mill. Disciples had disdained structure on the American frontier in the early 1800s. Like the New Testament church that anticipated Jesus' imminent return, Disciples naively expected Christians in America quickly to see the wisdom of a simple and uncomplicated faith that allowed for freedom of opinion about things theological. That meant a quick reunion of Christians now separated from the old enmities of Europe.

Early Thoughts About Church Structure

Thomas Campbell had said in 1809 that the church on earth was "constitutionally one," certainly an affirmation of wholeness in structure. Both Campbell, in western Pennsylvania, and Barton W. Stone, in Kentucky, would have remained within the existing Presbyterian structures if they could have. When that was no longer possible—from the Presbyterian point of view—the Campbells organized a Christian "association" outside the denomination, and Stone developed an independent presbytery. Still feeling the need of official linkages, the Campbells associated with the Baptists for a time. Stone finally killed his presbytery and simply resolved to "sink into union" with the body of Christ at large.

In 1835, three years after the Disciples and Christians informally had united their movements, Alexander Campbell wrote in his *Millennial Harbinger* about a linkage that would be voluntary: "The relation between congregations and their overseers, at the local or national levels, should be considered as a covenant, a relation which would most effectively safeguard both order and liberty." The preamble to the restructure document 133 years later would be called precisely that—a covenant. And the document would try to provide both order and liberty, as he envisioned.

In 1849, the first general convention was held and the American Christian Missionary Society organized. One hundred fifty six delegates from 100 congregations in eleven states came together in Cincinnati, Ohio, and although Campbell wasn't there he was elected president of the convention. He had hoped for a "convention of messengers of churches, selected and constituted such by the churches—one from every church." But too many people came without credentials and the process broke down. Everybody who came finally was permitted to vote. The missionary society, while acceptable to Campbell, was far from what he had in mind in terms of church structure. It was the brainchild of D. S. Burnet, who presided over the first convention in the absence of Campbell. The agency principle involved individuals, not churches, banding together to meet need.

Two decades after the first general convention there was another attempt to organize a delegated body for the governance of national work. The effort was called the Louisville Plan. Essentially it set up a structure that was presbyterial in character, with congregational delegates represented in districts, district delegates represented in states, state delegates named to the national convention. It even called for a common fund to be distributed 50 percent to the district, 25 percent for state work and 25 percent for national. In the convention of 1870, there were 74 delegates from fourteen states. However, 600 visitors were permitted to participate and the voting representation broke down. The idea died gradually over the next few years as financial support reached a new low.

In 1917, under F. D. Kershner, a bicameral government of sorts was established with the creation of the International Convention as the general body in assembly and a Committee on Recommendations as the creation of the various states, the latter being the first place to which business items were sent but with the convention having final authority. The actions were advisory where they concerned the societies or agencies.

In 1923, the Disciples organized the Commission on Budgets and Promotional Relationships to do something about the competing campaigns for support of the various church causes that had grown up over the years. That concern eventuated in Unified Promotion in 1934, an elaborate agreement by which most of the state organizations and national institutions affiliated with the Disciples agreed voluntarily to give up their free-wheeling campaigning among the churches for funds in favor of a cooperative approach.

The Council of Agencies

After World War II—both World Wars having had a positive effect on helping Disciples coalesce their work—there appeared a Council of Agencies. The San Francisco convention in 1948 called for a commission to study how the church and its agencies could fulfill their mission to the fullest and in the most effective manner. The prime mover in that call was Harlie Smith, who with Wickizer later would organize the Panel of Scholars. Smith was born in the same small northwest Missouri town, Maryville, from which Wickizer came to the UCMS. As a former president of William Woods College and the president of the Disciples Board of Higher Education, Smith would join Wickizer as one of the pillars of restructure.

An economics professor and investment specialist, Smith was a founder of the Council of Protestant Colleges and Universities. During the mid-1960s he was vice-president of the National Council of Churches and chair of its Christian Education Division, which held copyright to the Revised Standard Version of the Bible. He was a warm individual and practical joker, self-deprecating in manner. He had a strong sense of the need for authority in the church and he deplored the fact that agencies and boards had been brought into existence and ultimately accepted by the church "without any explicit delegation of authority to discharge the tasks which the boards have undertaken."

The Council of Agencies first met February 6-8, 1950, and was a focal point of the push toward restructure from the start. Between July 8 and 12, 1957, in Chicago, a committee established by the Council of Agencies held a consultation under the chairmanship of Wilbur H. Cramblet, president of the Christian Board of Publication. At that consultation it was reported that seven states already had developed delegate conventions, a key element in any international reorganizing by Disciples. The move was activated again, as it had been at least four times earlier in the Disciples history, to bring the annual national meeting together as a delegate assembly rather than a mass meeting.

Wickizer Proposes A Structure

It was Wickizer's presentation to the Council of Agencies biennial meeting in Canton, Missouri, in 1958 in which the first real structure proposals came forth. At the Canton meeting Wickizer said his task simply was to offer his best thinking about an improved structure for the church at that particular moment. Disciples had made much of the fact that they were "free men in Christ," he said, speaking in a day before the advent of inclusive language and using the phrase for the launching of a principle: "The basic unit of fellowship and cooperation of these 'free men in Christ' is the local congregation and these 'free men' bring to the congregation a freedom that cannot be abridged. This is a fact which it seems to me we must always take into account when we are thinking of organizational structure for our brotherhood, a fact which we should not try to circumvent or to limit."

Later, when foes would attack the process of restructure, they would forget that Wickizer principle. Never was there any evidence that leadership of the restructure effort had designs of power over congregations. He continued: "I think in restructuring the brotherhood we must preserve the principle of voluntarism on the one hand but must magnify the principle of responsibility on the other." That was a principle upon which the vast majority of those involved in restructure operated throughout. It became the core of the *Design for the Christian Church (Disciples of Christ)*.

34

Wickizer did not stop with generalities. He launched into specifics that stimulated others and formed the bases of much that was to follow. A new structure should be formed around the International Convention of Christian Churches. He proposed an equal number of ministers, laymen and laywomen comprise the successor to the Committee on Recommendations, which would be the smaller body to do the assembly's deliberative work. The general agencies could keep their corporate identities, suggested Wickizer, but boards would need to be elected by the total church rather than be self-perpetuating.

The UCMS and any other "societies" would need similarly elected boards rather than individual memberships. Wickizer called for the merging of financial structures in much the same manner as ultimately occurred. He concluded: "For too long we have been willing to add patch on patch, never moving according to a carefully worked out master plan. I believe the mood of our people would support such an undertaking at this time."

The Ball Begins to Roll

Wickizer's proposal struck a chord. The moment would be remembered long after by many of the principals as the launch-pad of restructure. Just a couple of months after the Council of Agencies speech, the International Convention named a Committee on Brotherhood Structure (not REstructure) and Wickizer was the chair. The committee was charged with exploring the magnitude and complexity of reorganizing the church and with formulating a proposal as to how a broadly representative commission on restructure might be constituted.

In the snowy hill country of southern Indiana, the committee on structure met at the quaint Canyon Inn of McCormick's Creek State Park January 7-9, 1960. At that meeting the decision was made to recommend appointment of a restructure commission to design a major organization shift for Disciples. To underscore the broad support of the change, two powerful state secretaries made the motion and the second in favor of the recommendation. They were Loren Lair of Iowa and Lester Rickman of Missouri, strong Disciples states. Both men were to become important figures in the restructure process.

The 111th annual session—dating back to the 1849 Cincinnati

convention—of the International Convention of the Christian Churches (Disciples of Christ) convened in Louisville, Kentucky, October 21, 1960. Twenty-nine agencies reported on their activities for the previous year. Resolutions were adopted that complained about indecent motion pictures and misleading liquor advertising, that supported the National and World Councils of Churches against attack, and that objected to a Louisville hotel and restaurant turning away black Disciples. The structure committee report took note that "piecemeal" restructure already was in process, including a UCMS internal reorganization, unification of work at the state level, and the unifying of promotional and planning processes at the national level.

The Wickizer committee's report attempted to allay any concerns that a restructuring might turn the Disciples inward and away from their Christian unity heritage. But the attempt became ammunition for those who would attack the restructure process half a dozen years later. The report said that restructure would provide a realistic update of the church's historical perspective "with a view to placing us in a stronger position to negotiate with other religious bodies that may be interested in discussing union with us." The convention's committee on recommendations tried to tone the phrasing down, making it simply "restructure should place us in a stronger position" rather than having it sound like an objective. But the linkage of restructure with the notion that Disciples were being prepared for merger with another denomination wouldn't go away.

The Commission on Brotherhood Restructure

When the Louisville convention approved the report in 1960, it authorized the appointment of a commission consisting of 120-130 persons and an effort at searching the real breadth and depth of restructuring the denomination. The convention approved a Central Committee of 18 persons (later increased to 25) to meet four to six times a year to do the heavy groundwork for the commission itself. The following February, George Earle Owen, loaned by the UCMS to administer the restructure commission, began contacting persons recommended by the International Convention board of directors. Edith Evans of Austin, Minnesota, wrote in her diary: "Asked to be on the restructure commission but don't believe I'll accept." She didn't remember what changed her mind but when the Commission on Brotherhood Restructure held its first meeting October 29-November 1, 1962, in St. Louis she was there, writing in the diary: "A full day of meetings. Looks as if this restructure is going to take several years."

The Commission on Brotherhood Restructure—125 members—was elected to three-year terms by the Los Angeles convention in 1961. Granville Walker was the chairman. He had been president of the International Convention when Wickizer made his 1958 speech. The 125 were well aware of the enormous task before them. They were also aware that they had been chosen to singularly important positions.

There were 91 ministers and 34 lay persons in the group. Seventeen women were sprinkled among the 108 men. Twenty were educators. Ten were agency executives. All but 30 came from large congregations of 500 members or more. The sensitivities to ethnic minority representation that marked the '70s and '80s had not been kindled at the outset of the '60s. Four blacks, no Hispanics and no American Asians were included.

The first commission meeting in St. Louis' Statler Hotel largely was devoted to orientation to the task. In calling for action on restructure, Wickizer observed: "As a brotherhood we have always found it easier to create new coordinating bodies than actually to restructure our organizational life and thus eliminate overlapping and competition at its source." Seminary dean Ronald Osborn announced that a denominational structure was not inconsistent with New Testament practices: "If the earliest Palestinian congregations could model their organizations and worship on the pattern of the Jewish synagogue, if Paul could argue for the financial support of the ministry on the basis of the wages paid to Roman soldiers, if the words of Jesus were translated and collected in Greek with the result that his original Aramaic utterances are lost except for a few words, theology can readily deduce the principle that as an institution in history the church rightly uses appropriate instruments out of its historic context for the achievement of its purpose."

The Panel of Scholars reports, while not published in book form until the issuing of three volumes in 1963, were circulated earlier among the restructure principals. Since the reports were intended to be a review of Disciples theology in general, they covered far more than structure. Among the other opinions offered by the scholars that had a bearing on major concerns of the Disciples in the 1960s were: Evangelism may include social action; unity in Jesus Christ requires diversity, not uniformity; radical individualism is not the Disciples' idea of liberty.

But the primary value of the Panel of Scholars reports was to say to Disciples: Practical churchmanship may be the heritage and style of Disciples of Christ but to have some depth, to be able to answer questions about one's faith, requires theological thinking and debate. It was time for Disciples to begin.

* * *

"Stories of . . . exemplary individuals are an important part of the tradition that is so central to a community of memory."

It was mid-1961 and ROSA PAGE WELCH was stunned and thrilled. At age 61, she had just been asked if she would like to go to Africa as a missionary—one of her lifelong ambitions. For 27 years she had given her talent as a soul-stirring mezzo-soprano not only to her own church, the Disciples of Christ, but to the whole Christian family.

She was more widely known, perhaps, than any other Disciple. But it was not without a price. She spent most of her time away from her husband and two children in Chicago. She sang and she spoke more than a hundred times some years. She faced the pressure of representing blacks constantly before white people ranging from presidents to prisoners. She suffered indignities everywhere she went, North and South, of not being permitted in hotels or in mixed company—outrages that were commonplace then, but difficult for people in the 1980s even to imagine. And she had to live with suspicion from many blacks who couldn't understand why she spent so much time with whites.

"I have always felt," she wrote in her autobiography, *Rosa's Song*, "that I was not representing just Rosa Page Welch but was representing every black person in America. What happened to me wasn't nearly as important as what could happen to the white people by my having a Christ-like attitude." She capped her philosophy—and theology—with the disarming observation: "You can love hate out of people."

Now she was being asked by the Church of the Brethren to

spend two years as a missionary in a remote part of Nigeria. She went alone for two years; her husband, a choir director and meat-packing employee, needed to keep the family together and explained with tongue in cheek that there were snakes out there. It was a memorable experience for Mrs. Welch, lonely at the outset, finding it difficult to sleep at first under a thatched-roof that might harbor "varmints."

She sang to lepers and tuberculars, chided African men for the way they treated their women, taught music, worried about her grandchildren and the state of race relations in the United States, and talked about the love of God and the Christian life, making skin tingle with that incredible voice, "There is a balm in Gilead . . ."

Rosa Page was born in Port Gibson, Mississippi, not far from the Mississippi River and midway between Vicksburg and Natchez, just after the turn of the century. Her great-grandfather was burned to death saving her father from a barn fire set by whites trying to take away their property. Her mother came from a sharecropper family. Her father was a barber and undertaker's assistant but he also was a tenor and a fiddle player who had his own band.

Father died when she was 16 and she and her mother became the janitors at the Christian Church. Since blacks were only afforded two years of high school those days, she applied to Southern Christian Institute in Edwards, some 35 miles away between Vicksburg and Jackson. She could earn her way through the famed institution begun by the Christian Church (Disciples of Christ). SCI was to produce many of the Disciples' prominent black leaders and would become the center of the Delta Ministry of the National Council of Churches during the civil rights struggles of the 1960s.

Noting the youngster's great voice, the school arranged through a wealthy woman in Chattanooga to underwrite voice training. A teacher helped her purchase a piano. Africa missionaries who visited the school inspired her to be a missionary. But it was famed blues singer Bessie Smith who appeared in a show in Port Gibson whom she credits for inspiration to become a concert singer.

She taught voice and piano in black schools in Mississippi and Kentucky, won some singing awards, and married in Chicago at age 26. At age 30 she had two children and had attracted the attention of an executive of the United Christian Missionary Society by winning a singing prize in the Chicagoland Music Festival. She was recommended as song leader for a student conference in Nebraska and that was the beginning of a quarter century of trying to help white people get to know blacks through her attention-getting talent and sharing of love.

The 1930s-50s were a prepping time for the civil rights revolution. The old racial separations, exclusions and injustices were still legal and still very much a way of life. Liberal-thinking people were looking for opportunities to bring whites into a better understanding of blacks in the hope that the barriers would begin to fall. Conferences of young people were particularly good places to begin the change. Rosa Page Welch was a godsend toward that objective.

Her conversions of white people to a better understanding of blacks were as legendary as her singing performances and the injustices she suffered traveling in white society. Youth conferences were shifted to other towns or held up until whites opened their lodging doors—not by Mrs. Welch but by the promoters of the experiences. She won over audiences who came not knowing she was black and would have barred her if they had known. She sang in an Indiana town where the courthouse land was to revert to original owners if a black person stayed overnight within the community. Somehow the town survived.

She posed as a nanny to gain entrance to a restaurant with white companions both to ease their embarrassment over her being blocked and to teach them what a trial it was for blacks to travel. She confronted a famous missionary with his racism when he spoke of the danger of white women walking in black neighborhoods, saying the reverse is more dangerous: "That's why we have so many light-skinned Negroes!" She forgave in loving embrace a minister's wife who years earlier had treated her with obvious contempt. She sang from a balcony when church elders ruled no black would stand in the chancel, winning them to a change of heart with her powerful and loving witness. She brought tears to the eyes of her audience after one difficult housing struggle when she rose to sing *The Holy City*: "All who would might enter and no one was denied."

The United Christian Youth Movement, United Church

Women (now Church Women United), the Disciples, the Presbyterians, the Brethren, and other church denominations and organizations engaged her continually in the task of song leading, performing and undermining racism from the mid-1930s well into the civil rights revolution of the 1960s. Much of her work was overseas, even before the 1961-63 missionary service. She spent seven months as an "Ambassador of Good Will" from a consortium of churches in the 1950s, visiting 18 countries on three continents.

Along the way: Mrs. Welch was awarded the Distinguished Service Medal from the National Conference of Christians and Jews. She was the song leader at the founding meeting of the National Council of Churches. She led singing at the Disciples' International Convention. She was in the first edition of *Who's Who Among American Women*. She was the first non-member of the Church of the Brethren to serve on that denomination's board. She was awarded an honorary Doctorate of Humane Letters by Eureka College. She was named an honorary member of Sigma Gamma Rho sorority, something that she was particularly proud of because it came from blacks.

After her Nigeria missionary service she worked for a time for the Disciples Unified Promotion (Church Finance Council) interpreting the church's mission. She worked two weeks in Hattiesburg, Mississippi, with the civil rights movement at the same time three young civil rights workers from the north were found murdered. Then she marched at Montgomery. In 1966 at the Disciples International Convention in Dallas, there was a resolution calling for an end to laws prohibiting interracial marriage. When whites seemed to be doing all the talking, Rosa Page Welch demanded attention and asserted, "White people think the Negro (It was before that word became out of favor) has nothing to say on this. I'd like to point out that there are very few pure Negroes in America today. In skin color the Negro comes in all shades from pure white to nearly pure black and this is not all our fault. It is the symbol of the aggression of white men on Negroes, not of Negroes on the white race. The whites have no objection to intermixture. They object only to legalizing it. This is an insult to the Negro race. But I don't think I am bitter toward you because of this. I decided long ago to put aside bitterness. No one is going to make a sinner out of me! You are my brothers, and I love you all whether you like it or not!"

3

Blueprint for Identity

1963—Fiers assumes restructure role part-time (Jan. 1) . . . Disciples send first delegation to COCU at Oberlin, Ohio (March 19-21) . . . *National Council calls churches to justice struggle* (June 7) . . . *Supreme Court rules against school prayer* (June 17) . . . Disciples organize moral and civil rights coordinating committee (June) . . . Covenant suggested at second restructure meeting (June 29-July 1) . . . *King's "I have a dream" speech* (Aug. 28) . . . Restructure workshop packed at Miami convention (Oct. 11-16) . . . *President Kennedy assassinated* (Nov. 22) . . . *Betty Friedan's* Feminine Mystique *published*.

1964—*3 Civil rights workers murdered in Mississippi* (June 22) . . . *Civil Rights Act passed* (June 29) . . . Fiers succeeds Cook as convention executive (July 1) . . . *Gulf of Tonkin incident opens Vietnam combat* (Aug. 7) . . . *Congress OKs War on Poverty bill* (Aug. 11) . . . Disciples couple to Mississippi for rights work for 15 months (September) . . . Detroit convention hears proposal for delegate assembly (Oct. 2-7) . . . 1,930 Disciples commit to direct action in race crisis.

The zenith of President Lyndon Baines Johnson's political career may well have been June 29, 1964. It was the day the omnibus Civil Rights Act passed. A Texan whose commitment to civil rights was suspect until he became President, the Disciples of Christ member championed the legislation that was considered among the most significant civil rights laws since the Civil War. The Rights bill banned racial discrimination in voting, jobs and public accommodations—putting the power of the federal government solidly behind civil rights. The President's War on Poverty program followed in legislation that year.

Johnson, having succeeded the assassinated President Kennedy a year earlier, was elected in the fall of 1964 to a term in his own right. However, it was mostly downhill for the President after that as he became mired in the Vietnam War. What much later was found to be a fabricated attack on an American naval vessel in the

Gulf of Tonkin off Vietnam put the United States into combat in that long and divisive war for the first time. Johnson's popularity plunged as both the war and the protests mounted. On March 31, 1968, he announced his intention not to seek reelection, knowing it was a lost cause.

The President had considerable help from the Disciples of Christ on the legislation that may have been his career high point. The church's Coordinating Committee on Moral and Civil Rights recruited 561 ministers to press for the Civil Rights Act of 1964, wrote 3,400 personal letters at various stages of the legislation, sent special mailings to ministers in 11 states, sent staff to work with churches in Iowa and Ohio, and visited Congress members in Washington.

Johnson was baptized as a youth by the Disciples of Christ in the Pedernales River in his hometown of Johnson City, Texas. The small, white frame Christian Church there bears a bronze marker placed by Disciples in 1975. His widow, "Lady Bird," and other members of the Johnson family were present as the marker was installed on the building identifying it as the President's boyhood church.

As President, Johnson attended church regularly, sharing his presence widely among denominations—often the Episcopal Church of which his wife was a member. Sometimes he would appear at National City Christian Church, where he was listed as an "honorary elder" and where the minister, Dr. George Davis, was identified by the press as the "President's pastor." When Johnson died, January 22, 1973, the nation watched the televised memorial service at the National City church, which is located just six blocks from the White House.

The National City church, under an earlier name, was the church of President James A. Garfield as well. Garfield was a Disciples of Christ preacher and college president (Hiram, in Ohio) 83 years earlier. The church was one of the places Garfield's assassin said he stalked the President but was afraid to fire in fear of hitting Garfield's mother. Ironically, the only other President of the United States to have been a member of the Disciples of Christ, Ronald W. Reagan, cited the problems of personal security as a reason for not attending church. Reagan maintained his membership in the Disciples' Hollywood-Beverly Christian Church,

Los Angeles, though he identified with the Presbyterian Church when he did attend during his political career.

Osborn Articulates the Concepts

The same day that President Johnson's Civil Rights Act passed in mid-1964, the Commission on Brotherhood Restructure convened for its third annual session. The restructure commission spent part of its first two years developing a statement on "The Nature of the Structure Our Brotherhood Seeks." That statement listed seven aims: (1) structures rooted in Christ's ministry made known through scripture, (2) structures comprehensive in ministry and in mission, (3) structures by which congregations may fulfill their ministries, (4) structures that are responsibly interrelated, (5) structures that manifest both unity and diversity, (6) structures that seek to be ecumenical, and (7) structures faithful in stewardship.

The 1964 session in Louisville would be identified with Ronald Osborn as much as the 1958 Council of Agencies session was identified with Willard Wickizer. It was Osborn's three lectures at Louisville that brought focus to what commission members were thinking. He spoke on the calling of the church, the nature of the church and the building of the church—observing that unintentionally but not unprovidentially those three concepts picked up on the three elements of Thomas Campbell's Declaration that the church is "intentionally, essentially and constitutionally one."

Osborn, in his powerful presentations, posed a question to the now 126-member commission and promptly answered it: "What then is the character of our corporate life? It is something far more than a convention, far more than a policy of cooperation, far more than an association of churches. It is the church, as surely as any congregation is the church. It is not yet the whole church, but it is the church."

So the key concept upon which most of the restructure commission seemed to agree was an expression of church, not some intensified form of cooperation. The church of Jesus Christ on earth was one and the Disciples of Christ were an expression of it. As such the "brotherhood" agencies were a manifestation of the church, the state organizations were a manifestation of the church, and congregations were a manifestation of the church. It

45

was not going to be easy to convince all Disciples. There remained a large bloc who had misgivings about "church" beyond the local congregation. The pre-restructure committee had put the issue pejoratively in one of its reports: "As a religious body we have had almost no theology of Church beyond the local congregation. The Church was only the sum total of autonomous congregations and it was thought congregational autonomy should be protected and preserved at all cost. Therefore, if organization must be developed beyond the local congregation for pragmatic reasons, it should be kept weak and relatively ineffective." The result: built-in inefficiency, said the committee.

The Idea of Covenant Emerges

So exactly how could the new relationship be expressed? Part of the Disciples heritage was an anti-creedalism proclaimed in the words "No creed but Christ." Any statement of faith, whether demanded as a requirement for membership or not, would be suspect by many as a creed and therefore antithetical to the faith as Disciples knew it and preached it. The idea of a covenant began to emerge, a biblical covenant. Even a covenant or covenantal declaration would rankle some but no one could argue that a covenant was not biblical.

The Bible itself was divided into the Old Covenant (Testament) and the New Covenant. Although some people had difficulty understanding the special biblical meaning of a covenant, the covenant's role in relating people to each other as well as to God, the initiator of the covenant, was particularly biblical.

Once again Ronald Osborn provided the groundwork. He described six biblical covenants and said: "The covenant is intensely personal but never merely individual. Whoever binds himself in covenant of faithfulness with God also binds himself to God's people. It is that common covenant which makes the church. It is to a group of people what the good confession is to an individual. The covenant is something that God initiates. We cannot make the covenant; we declare or acknowledge it and its consequences."

Such a covenantal declaration might include: the Lordship of Jesus Christ, the relation of Disciples to each other, openness to the Holy Spirit, unity and wholeness of the church of Christ on earth, existence of the church through baptism and participation in the Lord's Supper, God's gift within the church of ministry and of scripture, and commitment to God and to each other. Here was Osborn's concept of covenant accompanied with the caution that covenant should never be used as a test of church membership. It was not a statement to be required of someone as a sign of her or his commitment to the Disciples.

The use of covenant on the ecumenical scene—such as Consultation on Church Union churches covenanting together to pursue union—helped make the term more familiar. The biggest difficulty for Christians unaccustomed to biblical language was in differentiating the biblical covenant from the contractual use of the word in legal affairs. A covenant in secular terminology was a contract between two people with each party agreeing to certain provisions and bound to it by law.

The biblical covenant was based on the ancient suzerainty treaty—a treaty between landowner and peasant. The master imposed the covenant and the peasant accepted it whether he liked it or not. The biblical scholars noted that God instituted the covenant with Abraham not as an equal but as God. Abraham *would* be the father of a great nation. As long as Abraham did certain things which God asked, then God would do certain things in return—such as give Abraham and his progeny the land of Canaan. Jesus, of course, wrote the New Covenant on the heart and sealed it with his blood. When Disciples ultimately adopted their covenantal declaration, it was not referred to as a covenant in the document, at least partly due to concern about possible legal implications of the word. It is known only as the "preamble" to the *Design for the Christian Church (Disciples of Christ)*.

Assignment of the Tasks

W. Barnett Blakemore, dean of the Disciples Divinity House at the University of Chicago, edited the Panel of Scholars documents and was outspoken in his favoring a more theological understanding by Disciples of their nature. He was assigned the task by restructure commission chairman Granville Walker of chairing the documents task force, which carried responsibility for preparing the covenantal statement. It was a perfect match to Blakemore's talent.

The 179-word covenant that Blakemore and his task force developed was presented for the first time at the 1966 Dallas convention almost in the same words as used by congregations in worship settings in the mid-1980s, a tribute to its durability as an expression of the relation of Disciples to God and to each other. There was an adding of inclusive language, reversing the order of a couple of lines, printing it in poetic style for worship use and titling it the "Preamble," instead of "Introduction."

Otherwise, the covenantal declaration seemed to stand the test for Disciples. Blakemore encouraged congregations to formulate their own statements of faith as well—explaining that the exercise itself was profoundly rewarding.

Like the ancient suzerainty treaties, the Disciples' covenantal statement opened with an acknowledgement of who the parties to the covenant are, using the simple confession common to Disciples, "We confess that Jesus is the Christ, the Son of the Living God." Then followed an acceptance of the bond of the covenant, praise to the suzerain, and the statement of the bond of members to each other and "with the whole people of God." Then the particular symbol of the bond that is so especially oriented to the Disciples of Christ: "At the table of the Lord we celebrate with thanksgiving the saving acts and presence of Christ." The acknowledgement of gifts that have been the result of the bond: ministry and scripture. And finally the promise and sealing of the covenant. "In the bonds of Christian faith we yield ourselves to God that we may serve the One whose kingdom has no end. Blessing, glory and honor be to God forever. Amen."

Seven special task committees in addition to Blakemore's on basic documents formulated the concepts of restructure. Osborn chaired theological evaluation. James A. Moak, Kentucky state secretary, drew program structures. Spencer P. Austin, executive secretary of Unified Promotion (now Church Finance Council), headed promotional structures. Jo M. Riley, an Illinois pastor, was in charge of local church structure. Foreign missions executive Virgil A. Sly led ecumenical relations. The Kansas City Christian Church Commission's executive Harrell A. Rea was the chair of the restructure participation meetings task committee. Leslie R. Smith, a Kentucky pastor, chaired the nature and authority of the International Convention group.

A Straw Vote on Straw Votes!

A. Dale Fiers, of course, was the staff person. For the powerful figure that he was, he went about his work quietly. Never domineering, precisely organized, he evoked participation. He could be stubborn. Granville Walker presided over the commission with firmness, yet with a sense of humor that dissolved many moments of tension. He was effective and patient, a commission member said. Osborn described Walker's presiding as being with grace, intelligence and good humor. The humor was critical to a commission undertaking such a mind-stretching and belief-threatening task.

Black convention executive Emmett J. Dickson was a tension breaker, as was Harlie Smith, president of the Board of Higher Education. Robert A. Thomas, then a Seattle pastor, couldn't believe it when somebody wanted to take a straw vote on whether there should be straw votes! D. Wayne Doolen, a Montana accountant, recalls that when different drafts of the same paper were circulated accidentally, someone dubbed them the "wise and foolish versions." Attorney David Nelson Sutton of West Point, Virginia, became exasperated with the insertion of "weasel words" into documents and he thundered: "What do you suppose would have happened to this country if Patrick Henry had proclaimed 'Give me liberty and/or death?'"

Ronald Osborn estimates that the decisions of the commission were guided by about 15 percent of the body. The theologians and bureaucrats were the most outspoken. George H. Wilson, a Disciple serving the federation of churches in New Orleans, remembers being overawed coming into the setting once a year when some on the commission were living with it daily, but he felt that a democratic mode prevailed nevertheless and that every idea got its chance on its own merits. There were the inevitable clashes. Commission members remember Blakemore and Atlanta pastor Robert W. Burns, who had strong reservations about restructure, trading scriptural quotes on the floor. Rhodes Thompson, Jr., at 35 one of the youngest commission members, was cornered by ecumenical officer George Beazley in the rest room and lectured in no uncertain terms about how Disciples always had "ordained" their elders.

When mid-1965 arrived, Kenneth Teegarden became the first

full-time restructure administrative secretary, easing the load on convention executive Fiers. The restructure commission had voted unanimously in 1964 to ask Teegarden, who was Arkansas state secretary and who had written a constitution for Disciples there. Dale Fiers and Jessie Trout visited him in Little Rock. He turned them down. Too much was left to be accomplished in Arkansas. The commission next approached Harrell A. Rea, Kansas City Christian Church Commission executive and a restructure task force chairman. He also said no. Dale Fiers went back to Teegarden. "Don't you think this is the most important thing the church is doing? I did it for two or three years, giving up the presidency of the UCMS." The arm-twisting brought the Arkansas executive to Indianapolis.

Teegarden, a native of Cushing, Oklahoma, was the perfect choice. He had been a champion college debater at Phillips University and had thought about law as a profession. He was a stickler for detail, a crisp and precise writer—he loved crossword puzzles and he could finish one in an average of six minutes.

When a pastor still in his twenties he was thrust into the situation of organizing a city's religious response to one of America's worst tragedies; he was serving in Texas City and headed the ministerial association when harbor explosions killed 561 people on April 16, 1947. He was in Little Rock when the school integration crisis hit and was called upon to help direct the religious community's efforts to bring reconciliation. All of this stood him well for the restructure task.

A Structure Uniquely Disciples

As might be imagined, the form of government for the restructured church was a much-debated issue. If there were "manifestations" of the church beyond the congregation, would there be two or three? Some opted for a total of four manifestations, arguing that in addition to the local and the general there needed to be a few large administrative regions and numerous smaller pastoral districts. The issue was decided in favor of three, mainly because it was closer to what then existed. That issue returned in the 1980s with some renewed hope for a fourth manifestation in smaller districts or areas.

The concept of structure at the general manifestation was most easily equated to that of the congregation, with which everybody was familiar and most were comfortable. The congregation includes everybody and may meet only once a year on a regular basis, more often on call. The official board makes decisions within boundaries established by the congregation. The church cabinet administers those decisions in day-to-day operation. Internationally, a similar structure called for a General Assembly, a General Council and an Executive Committee. In the debate the latter two were changed to General Board—"board" being the more "Disciples" term—and Administrative Committee, which seemed to give a little less authority to the smaller body, a protection desired by many.

The commission overwhelmingly rejected the idea of a General Assembly that would not give congregations direct access. While a representative body was much desired—and would be the first action of the Disciples, preceding the restructure vote by two years—there was something participatory about the congregational polity that would be lost in a structure similar to many other churches, one in which congregations send delegates to a regional body and the regional body sends to the national. The upshot was the proposal for a combination of mass meeting and representative body. Congregations would send voters direct. Regions would send voters too. All Disciples would be invited to participate and would have full floor privileges except the vote. The General Board would be the principal deliberating body since the thousands at General Assembly hardly could have adequate debate time.

These and other issues occupied not only the annual meetings of the commission during the 1962-68 period but the four to six sessions annually of the 25-member Central Committee and various sessions of task committees. The result would be a structure uniquely "Disciples" in character. The covenant and new understandings of the church began to demonstrate the need for a change of terminology among Disciples.

Some historic terms, like "brotherhood," would die hard. Outsiders, particularly the press, always had difficulty understanding "brotherhood"; many equating it with a men's organization. Some uses could get downright amusing. Even before people were properly sensitized to sexism, the Disciples' news bureau had identified Disciples in the heading of press releases in a rather suggestive way: "A brotherhood of 5,000 congregations with relations with sister churches around the world"!

* * *

"Stories of . . . exemplary individuals are an important part of the tradition that is so central to a community of memory."

"The air was electric," she remembered about the experience of drafting a covenant through which Disciples could express their restructure. MAE YOHO WARD, the Disciples leading woman mission figure, was one of the members of the restructure commission's task force on basic documents who gathered in the Pension Fund offices in downtown Indianapolis to help Disciples state what their restructure was all about. W. Barnett Blakemore, dean of Disciples Divinity House at the University of Chicago, chaired the group. "Blakemore suggested we each write a statement as we would like to have it presented. I think it was an hour or more as we each wrote, looked out of the window, sat in deep thought, etc. The morning was over so we had box lunches brought in. Then Barney [Blakemore] read each statement thoughtfully and slowly. We had each written practically the same thing. The air was electric with our astonishment (and I felt with the Holy Spirit) . . . Barney said if he could be remembered for one thing he would like to be remembered for this statement of his faith, and I replied, 'I would be glad to settle for that too.'"

Mae Ward was someone who was in close touch with the Holy Spirit. Despite her mission management skills, her public speaking ability and her worldwide reputation, it was her spirituality that attracted people to her. Mae Ward was in touch with God. For 20 years the Latin America secretary of the Disciples' United Christian Missionary Society, Mae Yoho Ward was elected in 1961 to succeed Jessie Trout as vice-president of the Society. Nearly two decades (1951) before liberation theology came in vogue, Mae Ward had written that Latin America would have a role to play in the developing world community. "If its people are to make their rightful contribution to that community they need something more than a ritualistic, formal religion, unrelated to life and human relationships. They, as well as all the rest of the world, need to learn that when Christ told us to do good unto them that despitefully use us and to pray for them that curse us he was not inventing a method of behavior that he thought might have satisfactory results. He was making a statement about

52

reality—a statement that is a true one: that evil evokes evil, and good, good; and that good, if it is strong enough, overcomes evil." She criticized the "inability or unwillingness" of the church to deal with basic social problems of Latin America.

Mae Ward was born in 1900—a pastor's daughter—in the hills of West Virginia just a few miles south of Bethany, the historic college and home of Alexander Campbell. She attended Bethany College and then Yale University. She worked for a time as a public school teacher in West Virginia and then was director of religious education for the Disciples of Christ in the state. At age 28, she and her husband Normal Ward went to Argentina as missionaries. The missionary service lasted six years and Mae's marriage ended in divorce. They had one child, a son Don. She served briefly in Ohio and then at age 41 moved to Indianapolis where she was elected executive secretary for Latin America by the UCMS.

When she first came to the UCMS she initiated the unique practice of turning over the balance of her checking account each month, beyond her tithe, to the Disciples for their world work. She continued that until the UCMS management asked her to stop. She made friends around the world, working with the National Council of Churches, and speaking in churches everywhere. She was an excellent speaker.

As vice-president of the UCMS she made it her business to know the names of all of the employees—more than 200 of them—working in the church offices at 222 South Downey. And when new staff, at whatever level and with whatever agency, came to work at 222, she invited that person to dinner with key executives of the church at her tiny pink bungalow across a side street from "Missions Building," the name generally used to discribe the Disciples headquarters.

After a busy office day with mind-numbing policy decisions, she was the sole preparer of the dinner. That was a rule. And when new young couples were part of the guest list, she paid the babysitter, knowing that many of them could ill afford it. She led prayers and discussion with her guests, also involving them in natural ways in theological talk. Then came table games in which she was enormously competitive.

At her memorial service in 1983, Thomas J. Liggett, who had served as last president of the UCMS as a program unit, said that people who went to her home calling her "Dr. Ward" or "Mrs. Ward" always left addressing her as "Mae."

She had a strong feeling about social justice. She represented the Disciples in marching with the farm workers in California. She helped with the registration of black voters in Mississippi in 1964. She was a consultant at the Evanston Assembly of the World Council of Churches and a delegate to the New Delhi Assembly.

She wrote many letters, long letters. Very personal letters. Her prayer life was admirable. She always was first at the daily staff chapel in Missions Building. After she died, her prayer diary was excerpted into a book called *The Seeking Heart*, in which she poured out her faith uncertainties as well as her strong beliefs and trust. She disliked ostentation and she would greet it with her favorite expression, "Oh, for goodness' sake!"

Mae Ward retired in 1967, but immediately went to work again for the Disciples Board (now Division) of Higher Education. She recruited faculty for a private church college registry. Once on an airplane she struck up a conversation with a seat mate. She found out that the seat mate was a teacher. Before the ride had concluded Mae had him on the college registry.

In her late seventies and suffering from cataracts, Mae Ward took on an additional role at her beloved Missions Building. She became the volunteer gardener for the grounds. She ignored comments that she was too old for the work, that she shouldn't be bending over after cataract surgery, and that it lacked dignity for a former vice-president of UCMS. Instead she maintained that since she had promised neighbors that the building and grounds always would look nice when she promoted addition of a new wing in 1958, she was going to keep that promise.

In 1975 she was the Garrison Lecturer at Yale Divinity School and she used the occasion to speak about women's liberation. When women are fully liberated, she said, men will have fewer heart attacks. Women will be less inclined to load husbands with their ambitions. "Most women feel valued only as they win favor in the eyes of a man and are of worth only as he is accepted and successful in the community." Liggett deliberately referred to her in a eulogy as "very unique"—an expression she once criticized as ungrammatical. Sometimes, he said, it takes bad grammar to tell a truth. Mae Ward was very unique!

4

The Search for Consensus

1965—35,000 in restructure meetings in 82 locations . . . *King arrested in Selma* (Feb. 1) . . . *Marines sent to Dominican Republic* (Apr. 28) . . . COCU meets at Lexington (April 5-8) . . . Teegarden becomes restructure secretary (June 1) . . . *Combat missions begin in Vietnam* (June) . . . *China cultural revolution begins . . . Watts riot kills 34* (Aug. 11) . . . International Convention divides to 13 locations for restructure dialogue (October).

1966—UCMS staff supports phase-out under restructure (Jan. 27) . . . *First artificial heart developed* (Apr. 21) . . . *U.S. Forces begin firing into Cambodia* (May 1) . . . COCU okays principles of church union (May 5) . . . *Bombing of Hanoi begins* (June 29) . . . 3rd Quadrennial held (June 30) . . . *Medicare takes effect* (July 1) . . . Dallas convention adopts representative assembly (Sept. 23-28).

It was a moment that Barton W. Stone, resting peacefully nearby under the trees these many years, would have appreciated. In the old log Cane Ridge Meeting House near Paris, Kentucky, during the spring of 1965, a communion service was in progress. It was a typically Disciples service. But the participants—in addition to Disciples—were Methodist, Presbyterian, Episcopalian, United Church of Christ, and Evangelical United Brethren.

Those same rolling hills adjacent to that same building 164 years earlier had served as natural pulpits for Methodist, Presbyterian and Baptist preachers for a Friday-till-Wednesday "Cane Ridge Revival." It was the religious Woodstock of the day. The claim is that 20,000 people were there. That would have been a tenth of the population of the state of Kentucky. Barton Stone used the occasion to demonstrate the power of Christians when they were preaching the word as "Christians" and not on behalf of some denominational loyalty.

In 1965 Stone lay 30 feet away under a headstone while another singular ecumenical event was taking place. For these delegates to the fourth annual session of the Consultation on

Church Union, being held in Lexington, it was a mystical moment to be breaking bread together in this cradle of Christian unity. The four churches that Presbyterian Blake mentioned in his 1960 San Francisco sermon indeed had responded to the call, and in 1962 COCU was born. The Disciples and the Evangelical United Brethren, already in union conversations with the United Church of Christ and the Methodists respectively, were invited, had accepted (the Disciples by action of their convention in the fall of 1962), and now the foursome was six. Barton Stone not only was one of the progenitors of the Disciples of Christ but was the forbear as well of the Christian Churches that were subsumed in the United Church of Christ.

For many of the COCU delegates it was the first time to be served the Lord's Supper by lay persons. Cleveland lawyer Oliver Schroeder was one of the elders, a man from the church in Paris the other. George G. Beazley Jr., president of the Disciples Council on Christian Unity and one of the most widely-visible ecumenists in the world, presided from the old pulpit, facing the ancient wooden pews and the slave balcony above.

Beazley was one of the Disciples' most fascinating personalities of the period. He had come to the unity position from a pastorate in Bartlesville, Oklahoma, and he took his calling as seriously as anyone ever did. He traveled constantly in ecumenical circles. A Methodist bishop once said that he could be anywhere in the world, look up, and there would be George Beazley. Short, stocky and round-faced, he always wore a coat and tie and he was the epitome of an intellectual. His wife, Charlotte, traveled with him everywhere and they could be heard reading aloud to each other inside their hotel room. His camera was with him always and he took 35,000 color slides, many of them of art objects. He wrote a candid ecumenist's journal called *Beazley Buzz* in which he rambled through a description of his gall bladder surgery one moment and a discussion of Voltaire, Rousseau and Calvin the next—the latter tossed off lightly but with such insight that it set leading ecumenical colleagues abuzz.

Beazley would be elected to chair the Consultation on Church Union in the March 9-13, 1970, St. Louis session in which a plan of union would be completed and sent to the churches. He would finish his service in the chair April 2-6, 1973, in Memphis as COCU set a new direction for itself. Six months later he would die suddenly, still in his mid-50s, while dining with Charlotte in a Moscow hotel. The tenderness with which the Russian Orthodox Church would handle the situation, providing Charlotte with an around-the-clock English-speaking companion, would endear the Orthodox forever to the Disciples.

The Lexington meeting debated issues of ministry and brought the COCU delegates (nine from each church) to the point where they felt ready to have a commission begin drafting a possible plan of union. Significantly, in a statement to all the churches following the meeting, the COCU delegates referred to the "providential" nature of their being in Cane Ridge where, the Consultation said, one of the climactic and powerful events in the history of American Christianity took place.

Said COCU: "Here, in the early years of the Republic, God led many thousands of his people to see a new vision and find a new obedience. What they saw was a church simple, unified, scriptural, whole and true to the nature and mission of the great church. It is our prayer that such a vision may be given us and our companions and so we be led to the obedience to greatness God requires of us."

Paul A. Crow Jr., 33 years old and a professor at Lexington Theological Seminary, had begun serving the prior year as volunteer associate executive secretary of COCU. For the church history specialist it was the beginning of an ecumenical service that would take him to the far reaches of the globe countless times and make him a world figure in ecumenical circles. When COCU established an office in Princeton, New Jersey, in 1968, Crow was called as the first fulltime general secretary. He served there through the development and study of a plan of union and the major decision to shift the union approach from a structured plan to a gradual ground-level growing process.

When Beazley died, Crow returned to his denomination as the ecumenical officer. He chaired a National Council of Churches committee that altered the character of that body, represented the Disciples on the Central Committee of the World Council of Churches and moderated the WCC's Ecumenical Institute, training young ecumenists at Chateau de Bossey in Switzerland. William Jackson Jarman, pastor in Illinois and then New York City, chaired the Disciples delegation through the early years, sitting on the COCU executive committee.

COCU Adds to Its Number

COCU grew between the April 5-8, 1965, Lexington meeting and the May 2-5, 1966, gathering in Dallas. The African Methodist Episcopal Church—one of three historic black Methodist bodies that eventually would be a part of COCU—joined in the fall of 1965. The following spring the Presbyterian Church U.S., or southern Presbyterians, moved into full participation. Both had been among the several churches with observer-participant status at COCU plenaries. Later the African Methodist Episcopal Zion Church and the Christian Methodist Episcopal Church, predominantly black bodies, and the National Council of Community Churches would join. With the uniting of the Methodists and Evangelical United Brethren (1968) and the two Presbyterian bodies (1984), COCU became a nine-member movement in the mid-1980s.

At Dallas in 1966, although there was heated debate over whether a united church should have bishops with appointive powers, the COCU delegates formalized their considerable agreement up to that point. Using the title "Principles of Church Union," the ecumenists sent out to the denominations for study their work on faith, worship, sacraments and ministry. One thing the delegates were quite certain about: God's church was one and they were called upon to do something about the human-made divisions within it. "God's will is resisted and denied" by the separations, the *Principles* said.

The delegates were quite affirmative on some of their other principles as well. The united church would give maximum protection to "existing diversity and liberties," recognizing that there is evidence of the one church in each of the denominations. The united church would be a "uniting" church as well. This union would be only the beginning of its task in seeking wholeness of the church. The Apostles and Nicene Creeds would be used, but "not to coerce or control" personal commitment. Baptism would be by the various forms and at the various ages used by the existing churches, but never "imposed contrary to conscience." The Lord's Supper would be at the heart of the church's worship and presided over by ordained persons. Finally, the ordained ministry would include bishops, presbyters (elders) and deacons, though the COCU delegates professed not to be locked into the full functions of those offices.

The Critical Dallas Convention

When the Disciples convened their International Convention four and a half months later in the same city, there was time scheduled on the program for discussion of COCU. That term "bishop" unnerved many Disciples. The fear among Disciples was that bishops were dictatorial, placing ministers in congregations whether the congregations wanted them or not, and telling people what they should believe.

With that in mind, the Council on Christian Unity looked to a lay person of some credibility for interpretation help. Oliver P. Schroeder, a Cleveland lawyer who directed the law-medicine center at Western Reserve University, was chosen. He was a delegate from the Disciples to COCU and one of three lawyers who formed an informal panel to advise the union movement on the legal traps.

The group's most interesting advice came later when the plan of union was developed and the trio was asked to identify the possible legal snares. They came back with the surprising recommendation to proceed with full speed, noting that God's will should not be circumvented by the fear of the law. When legal snares come, then let them be dealt with.

At Dallas, Schroeder enthralled the convention with his humor and his debunking the stereotype of the power of bishops. Using the Episcopal bishop of Virginia, who at the time was chairman of COCU, and his own Ohio state secretary as examples, Schroeder exclaimed to a laughing and applauding convention: "If you think Bishop Gibson in Virginia has more power than Herald Monroe, you've got another think coming!"

The Dallas convention, which for restructure was a crucial test, nearly resulted in disaster. Key Dallas lay leadership objected strongly to the invitation to Martin Luther King Jr. to speak. King had been accused of links to international communism (a charge that troubled many Christians but a charge that much later was found to be a fabrication by the FBI to discredit the civil rights leader).

A fierce verbal battle ensued in which certain Dallas hosts threatened to pull their support of the convention and to torpedo restructure if King spoke. But A. Dale Fiers, the convention executive, and Stephen J. England, dean of the seminary at Phillips University and president of the convention, were adamant. The program committee wanted Dr. King, so Dr. King was going to speak at the Dallas convention.

Finally a compromise was struck. Two other speakers would share the platform with King, one being Pittsburgh Roman Catholic Bishop John J. Wright and the other, Dallas' own Robert G. Storey, a member of the Disciples and past president of the American Bar Association who was an opponent of civil disobedience. That did not ease the anger of some of the hosts, but it enabled the convention to go on as scheduled, and it made for one of the most powerful programs ever for a Disciples assembly.

More than 9,000 actually were in the arena that night, the largest single session attendance of the post World War II era. Security for King was tight since Dallas had witnessed the assassination of President Kennedy only a few blocks away some three years earlier.

The Dallas convention-goers got the first public look at a "Provisional Design" for the restructured church. But more importantly they voted on whether the Disciples thereafter would convene as a delegate assembly, an achievement that eluded Alexander Campbell and others of a similar bent for more than a century. "There never was a time that I felt the whole thing might come unglued," remembers Fiers. "But it hung in the balance as we approached the Dallas convention. A representative body. This was considered the first decisive step. If we failed, the restructure would be difficult."

The proposal called for an end to the mass assembly in which everybody who registered could vote. Instead, the people would send representatives. Since everyone else would be invited to participate as non-voters those things so grand about the mass assembly—the broad sense of involvement, the opportunity for education and inspiration, the experience of the wider church— would be preserved. When the Dallas convention was over, the restructure commission and the Disciples had their representative assembly.

Whether or not restructure was accomplished the Disciples would no longer be ruled at the national/international level by whoever could muster the most individuals at any given location. Congregations would be entitled to two voting representatives from the laity. Those with 751 or more participating members would have increased numbers. All ordained ministers would be given the right to vote. The other voters would be the 201 members from the Committee on Recommendations, all of whom were representatives of states and areas, and the 117 who would represent the agencies that received money through Unified Promotion.

The plan assured hat lay people would have the majority of the votes. As it worked out in practice over the next 20 years, whether the General Assembly attendance was 8,000 or 10,000, about half were voters and the other half non-voters. The breakdown of lay to clergy voters would hang consistently about 60-40 in percentage, laity predominating.

Opposition, Loyal and Otherwise

The fact that congregations now for the first time had a direct vote in matters concerning the world work of the church did not ease the perception among some people that congregations were under grave threat by the restructure moves. The restructure commission was shocked early in its work by the circulation of two pamphlets by an anonymous "Committee for the Preservation of the Brotherhood." The pamphlets warned of the dangers of the loss of local property in a restructured church.

Disciples leaders assailed the anonymous character of the pamphlets. Years later James DeForest Murch of Cincinnati, an Independent Christian Church historian, acknowledged writing the publications. Their distribution was funded by Pennsylvania oilman B. D. Phillips, also an Independent and donor of the headquarters building of the Disciples of Christ Historical Society in Nashville, Tennessee. Murch apparently felt the anonymity necessary, because his credibility would be suspect as an Independent standing to gain from frightened congregations defecting to the Independent cause.

Then there was the "loyal opposition." The central figure in it was Robert W. Burns, pastor of the Peachtree Christian Church, Atlanta, a member of the restructure commission and a former president of the International Convention. Burns' concern, a concern of others as well, was that local church autonomy not be compromised in any way. If the agencies of the church at the national and international level needed to be reorganized, so be it. But don't include the congregation in it.

Burns proposed in commission session that the language from the bylaws of the International Convention assuring that convention actions are purely advisory be carried over into the restructured church. He had been voted down. That was the basis of his fear that there was intent to draw a document that would bind a congregation's property to the denomination if that congregation should exercise its right to withdraw from the Disciples. He had been raising questions all along in the restructure commission but on May 4, 1967, he and others issued an Atlanta Declaration vowing to protect "the present brotherhood as a free association of congregations."

A Provisional Design for the Christian Church (Disciples of Christ)—the restructure document—drew strong fire from the Atlanta Declaration Committee. The proposed Administrative Committee in the Design, the Atlanta group said, would be an "ecclesiastical court." They objected to what they felt was a requirement that regions consult with the General Minister and President in naming their regional ministers.

The "order" of the ministry contained "hierarchical overtones" that point toward "ultimate ecclesiastic regimentation" through the power of the regions to certify ministers for standing. The document left Disciples open to being dragged into merger with other denominations. It allowed compromising of denominational principles in the interest of ecumenical ties, possibly "including even a recognition of the authority of the Pope."

There was an exchange of legal opinions. Burns wrote extensively to attorneys general in the United States and its territories. Kansas Disciples received an opinion from their attorney that appeared to support the opponents' worst fears. Nashville attorney William F. Carpenter, contacted by Burns, gave the opinion that the "language of the restructure agreement is dangerous, will be provocative of trouble and could and perhaps would result in congregations losing their property in the event dissension later arises."

A partner in the Cleveland law firm of Squire, Sanders and Dempsey, answering an inquiry from Ohio state secretary Herald Monroe, had just the opposite opinion: "It is apparent upon reading the *Design* that the commanding power rests with the congregation rather than with superior organizations or higher clergy. The emphasis throughout the *Design* is upon the voluntary association of congregations . . . It is difficult to imagine that congregational rights over their property—indeed their autonomy—could have been put in any clearer terms."

Seven members of the Central Committee of the restructure commission met with 17 members of the Atlanta Declaration Committee in Dallas, August 3, 1967. The Atlanta group insisted on the congregation retaining the power to determine the standing of its own minister in the total church. While restructure commission members agreed to spelling out better in the Provisional Design rights and safeguards for congregations, they were unwilling to have congregations certify their own ministers as qualified for service elsewhere in the denomination. And they would not bow to use of the word "autonomy" in the document. It was their conviction that no part of the body of Christ can be autonomous. Free, yes, but not autonomous. There were responsibilities to the larger Christian community.

Questions being raised by opponents like the Atlanta Committee caused restructure planners soon after the Dallas convention to move toward delaying the final vote one year. The decision was made that the 1967 St. Louis convention would simply commend the document. Then, while national/international agencies and the states and areas took separate actions to indicate their willingness to be a part of the restructured church, the convention staff would begin tooling up for final action and the first provisional General Assembly in Kansas City in 1968. Further, the delay would give everybody one more year to study and become comfortable with the idea.

The Campaign to Get Congregations to Withdraw

The 1965 *Year Book and Directory of the Disciples of Christ* listed 8,162 congregations. That was the peak number. The figure dropped by 15 in 1966. It fell 101 in 1967 and 2,106 in 1968—during the year of the restructure adoption. Two Illinois ministers were active in circulating forms for withdrawal from the book.

Most of the congregations that withdrew had been independent many years and simply had not taken the formal step of removing their names from Disciples records. It was true also that the listing of many congregations occurred without an action on

63

their part. Year Book listings began in an informal "brotherhood" era as simply someone's compiliation of congregations that had their origins in the Campbell-Stone movement.

Over the six-year period from 1967 to 1972, the *Year Book* declined by 3,538 congregational listings. Local offerings to the world outreach of the church increased by $1.3 million in the same period. The pain of the loss should not be minimized in the increase of dollars, however. There were a few historic congregations—like the one at Wellsburg, West Virginia, where Campbell and other luminaries of the movement preached—that had been cooperative and were drawn out by the fear tactics.

* * *

"Stories of . . . exemplary individuals are an important part of the tradition that is so central to a community of memory."

It was the mid-1960s and the five-year-old nation was aflame. The Belgian Congo, in process of becoming Zaire, instead seemed to be disintegrating from internal strife. Rebels were advancing from the east. Missionaries had been evacuated. Congolese, particularly the educated ones, were in great danger. Many had been killed.

The letter that BOKELEALE ITOFO BOKAMBANZA wrote to North America during that period showed a classic Christian courage and trust in God: "Today we have had news that Boende has fallen into the hands of the rebels and before long they will arrive here in Coq Mbandaka. I do not know what things will befall us in the days ahead. The Lord only knows. We have an opportunity to leave here and go on to Leo Kinshasa as others are doing, but you know that all of the Christians and the Catholics and those in authority are watching to see what I do. Therefore, we will stay here with all the others until the rebels arrive. I have asked Yoana to go if she wants to go but she does not want to leave me. She says if death awaits us, we will die together . . . So may the will of God be done. . . ." Government troops arrived in Mbandaka and stopped the rebel advance one day before it would have entered the city.

Bokeleale (pronounced Bo KAY lee AH lee) was 46 years old at the time. He was the new general secretary of the Disciples of

Christ community in the Congo, centered in the forests of Equator Province some 400 miles up the Congo river from the capital of Leopoldville (Kinshasa). A short, stocky man, he had five small, horizontal slash marks stacked neatly above the bridge of his nose. They were scars from his tribal youth. He had put them there with a knife, taunted by his 13-year-old friends.

For Bokeleale they were symbols of the past—symbols of a youth who learned to write with a stick in the soft earth of the forest; now he wrote and spoke in four languages. They were symbols of colonial days in the Belgian Congo; he was now a citizen of the soon-to-be Republic of Zaire. They were symbols of a day when the Christian faith was delivered by white people who came from afar; now the Congo church was a free church that preached the gospel to its own people in its own way.

Bokeleale was born in a small village near Lotumbe, where there was an historic Disciples mission station. He was of the Bombomba clan, the Mongo tribe and the Bantu ethnic group. His father was baptized by missionary H. C. Hobgood. To become a Christian the father gave up his other wives, chose one, and moved to the community of Christians around the church. "The church was a big family. This we could understand," said Bokeleale, who was then called by the French name Jean. The father died when he was quite young.

Hunting, fishing and building huts occupied the time of Congolese youths. Many times missionary preachers stopped overnight in Jean's home en route to Lotumbe. These visits and his mother's prayers were the boy's first remembrance of what it was like to be Christian.

Bokeleale was sent by his mother to the mission school in Lotumbe at 11. His grandmother, a non-Christian, promptly came and got him at night and took him home. He was 13 before he received a second start at education. He was an average student by his teachers' memories and his own confession. Six years later he entered Congo Christian Institute in Bolenge after having been baptized by Hobgood in the river. At the institute he first felt "obligated as a Christian." He finished his three years there and became a teacher, teaching at the institute for 15 years.

Virginia Clarke, a missionary, tutored him privately in English, math and French three nights a week and some Saturdays for two years because he came and begged her to help her learn. As a teacher, Bokeleale was held in high esteem by students and fellow teachers. He had a maturity about him that invited his counsel on discipline and student problems. He married the daughter of a Congolese evangelist who also was a product of the Lotumbe mission school.

A missionary recalled that one of his seven children, a three-year-old, carried a piece of chalk home from school one day. The next day he returned, held out his hand, and told a teacher, "I'm sorry, Mama, that I took the chalk. Please forgive me."

In 1956, the Congo church brought Bokeleale to Mbandaka to teach religion in four government schools. He was ordained at the same time by the Mbandaka church and became its associate pastor. Two years later he was invited to Brussels by the Belgian government to work with the Protestant mission exhibit in the Congo Building of the World's Fair. He remained in Belgium five years, studying at the Protestant Theological Seminary under a Disciples of Christ grant.

The Congo became a nation while Bokeleale was absent. He returned and not long after was named associate general secretary of the church, under missionary Richard Taylor, the top officer. He was in that associate position when the rebel uprising began in 1964. Bokeleale became the acting general secretary as the missionaries were evacuated.

In 1966, as hostilities ended, Bokeleale was named the first African general secretary of the Disciples church in the Congo. He tackled the assignment with enthusiasm. He was in the United States in 1967 and he held a prayer and orientation session at the Disciples' 222 South Downey Avenue offices in Indianapolis with a group of missionary doctors and wives who were enroute to his country. On October 13, 1968, one of the group, Eunice Goodall, and two other missionaries were killed when their light plane crashed in a storm between Mbandaka and Boende. The forest was so thick that the crash site wasn't discovered until Thanksgiving Day. Bokeleale suffered greatly, and the African church worked round the clock to locate the wreckage and minister to the families.

Bokeleale became the chief executive of the Congo Protestant Council and finally in 1970 the president of the Church of Christ in Zaire, a united body of more than 50 denominations and five times the size of the Disciples of Christ in North America. On

January 13, 1972, President Mobutu Sese Seko issued a decree sanctioning only three churches in Zaire—the Church of Christ in Zaire, the Catholic Church and an indigenous Christian body, the Church of Jesus Christ on Earth by the Prophet Simon Kimbangu. The sanction would bring with it virtually guaranteed growth under favored status but also the ambiguities of linkage to government and whether that involves compromises to the Christian witness.

To symbolize the new day in mission relationships, Bokeleale presented to the Division of Overseas Ministries in 1965 a three-foot-tall wood sculpture of a deer bending to nuzzle a fawn. He interpreted: The fawn was the African church, now old enough to stand on its own, with the continuing love between parent and child, but on its own. "I love the missionaries and it is because of their love I am able to do things. But we are no longer a mission. We are a church. You came to build a church. Let it be a church."

5

Framework for Identity

1967—*3 Mercury astronauts killed on pad* (Jan. 27) . . . Atlanta Declaration Committee organized (May 4) . . . *Six-day Egypt-Israel war ends* (June 5) . . . *Chinese test H-bomb* (June 17) . . . *Newark, Detroit race riots kill 66* (July 12-23) . . . *Marshall sworn in on Supreme Court* (Oct. 2) . . . St. Louis convention recommends Provisional Design (Oct. 13-18) . . . *Stokes, Hatcher elected in Cleveland, Gary* (Nov. 7) . . . *Barnard transplants heart* (December).

1968—Georgia first region to OK restructure (Jan. 16) . . . *North Korea seizes Pueblo* (Jan. 23) . . . *Tet offensive by North Vietnam* (Jan. 30) . . . Pension Fund, Christmount put restructure over the top (March) . . . *Martin Luther King assassinated* (April 4) . . . *Robert Kennedy assassinated* (June 5) . . . *Czechoslovakia invaded by USSR* (Aug. 20) . . . Black Disciples vote conventions merger (Aug. 25) . . . *Woodstock music festival* (August) . . . Kansas City convention votes to adopt restructure (Sept. 28).

The year that the Disciples of Christ chose to finalize their restructure—1968—was a tragic one. It was the year of the Communist Tet offensive in Vietnam, which brought more deaths, and more discouragement about the war. Martin Luther King Jr. was assassinated in April, triggering more race riots in the cities and disgust and discouragement in the churches. Then Senator Robert F. Kennedy, campaigning for the Presidency, was assassinated in June. The Democratic Convention was rocked by riots in Chicago. The Soviet Union invaded Czechoslovakia. Young people tried to escape it all—or capture the frustration—in the monumental music festival at Woodstock. Then in the fall a missionary airplane in Zaire crashed and killed three Disciples missionaries. It was the kind of time when issues of structure paled in importance.

Yet the timetable to restructure ran relentlessly to its conclusion. For months prior to the Kansas City Assembly the restructure action was in the board rooms of church agencies and in the state and area offices. Restructure required approval of two-thirds of the states and area associations of Disciples, and of two-thirds of the international and national agencies, as well as a two-thirds vote of the General Assembly. On January 16, Georgia Disciples became the first region to vote in favor of being a part of the restructured church, followed closely by Minnesota and the Dakotas. In March, the denomination's Pension Fund and Christmount Christian Assembly in North Carolina became the general agencies that put their manifestation over the two-thirds mark. As it turned out, all of the states and areas and all of the national/international agencies voted to participate in the restructured church.

The Saturday restructure vote at Kansas City, which, as indicated earlier, was followed by a standing ovation and the singing of the Doxology, was celebrated more fully the following Tuesday evening. Disciples convened their new General Assembly that night for a service of praise and thanksgiving. It was a memorable occasion. Osborn, the first Moderator, presided. Jean Woolfolk and Walter Bingham, the Vice Moderators, read scripture. The congregation included the World Council of Churches' general secretary Eugene Carson Blake from Switzerland, the chief executives of five American denominations, and the top officers of the American Bible Society and Religion in American Life.

New Structure Uncomfortable at First

The next few years would experience a great deal of uncomfortable shuffling about. The first few meetings of the 250-member General Board (annual) and the 44-member Administrative Committee of the General Board (three times annually) were exercises in confusion about authority and role. The pastors and lay people in both bodies were uncertain whether they could "direct" the former agencies to do anything and were not sure what data it was proper to request. The chief executives of the former agencies and now general administrative units likewise were not certain whether they were welcome at meetings of the plenary bodies (even though they officially were ex-officio non-voting members of the General Board) or how much they were permitted (or required) to participate.

The General Cabinet—a gathering of the presidents of the units and the general minister and president and his executive staff—wasn't even mentioned in the Provisional Design. That made a few Cabinet members nervous. One warned Dale Fiers, the general minister and president, not to consider Cabinet members his staff. Concerns about the Cabinet not being a decision-making body often caused it to deal with "safe" items of mechanics rather than the deeper issues of the church. It took a while for the general unit executives to begin thinking in terms of total church and to become comfortable with each other.

The regional ministers—some of them—felt left out even though they all were non-voting members of the General Board and there was a "Council of Ministers" annually, made up of regional ministers and the general unit presidents. Mistakenly, there was concern that the real action was taking place in Cabinet or the Administrative Committee. They no longer were all on the Unified Promotion (financing) board. And the permanent restructure follow-up committee, the Committee on Structure and Function, began getting pushy about regional realignment. In fact, whether the result of pressure or not, much of the restructure action was taking place in the regions shortly after the restructure adoption. The Conference of Regional Ministers and Moderators knew full well of the unevenness of the regional structures. Regions ranged in size from three congregations and 647 people to 466 congregations and 120,000 people. Realignment negotiations were numerous and within the next few years four new regions grew out of negotiations among nine. California South and Hawaii merged into the Pacific Southwest. Colorado and Wyoming became the Central Rocky Mountain region. Iowa, Minnesota and the Dakotas became the Upper Midwest. New Mexico and Texas inaugurated the Southwest region.

The basic problem in the regional church remained. Some were too small to be viable, a few perhaps even too large and unwieldy with districts that bid for power. But studies by the structure committee bent on showing optimum size and pressing for fewer and larger regions were annoying. The committee itself was showing some exasperation. At one session with regional ministers, Jean Woolfolk, as chairperson of the structure committee, reacted to calls for more study with: "Boys, study time is over. It's time for the final examination!" The fewer and larger push eventually was shelved as concern mounted that closer pastoral oversight of congregations may be needed more than administrative efficiency.

Congregations Hardly Touched

The fears of the restructure opposition that somehow congregations would be dominated certainly didn't materialize. The congregations were left untouched in restructure except for having gained a voting representation in the General Assembly, an impression that there would be less overlapping and more efficiency in the church's general work, and hopefully a heightened sense of identity and wholeness of church. Pastors in the mid-1980s seemed to feel there was little impact on their congregations from a restructure that took place more than 15 years earlier. Some confirmed that laity were aware of the church structure terminology, but others said their lay people were not even aware there were general structures. Some knew that a restructure took place but few knew what it was about. "It didn't impact the congregation," said a Missouri pastor flatly in 1986. Also, some of the so-called "big steeple" preachers lamented that after restructure they were no longer consulted as representative government took over, a fact that meant that some of the power of the stronger congregations was missing at the denominational level when it was most needed.

UCMS Leads the Way

The United Christian Missionary Society, in large measure, was the Christian Church (Disciples of Christ) world outreach prior to restructure. It owned and managed the major Indianapolis office building. It conducted overseas mission. It operated home missions. It provided services in women's work, men's work, Christian education, social action, evangelism and membership, ministry and worship, outreach education, print resources and audiovisuals. Forty percent of the church's giving beyond the congregation was administered through UCMS. It had a professional staff of 89 (the two divisions that succeeded it had combined staffs totaling 60 in 1986).

UCMS executives seemed prepared to show the way, whatever the society's vulnerability. Wickizer had been the chairman of one of its three divisions. Fiers was the president when restructure took shape. On January 1, 1963, he assumed part-time the administration of the restructure process. Fiers in 1964 moved full time to the position of executive secretary of the International Convention.

Virgil A. Sly, the long-time foreign division head and new president, took recommendations to the UCMS staff in January of 1966—two years before the restructure adoption—that included a phase-out of UCMS altogether as a program unit of the church and the establishment of separately-governed overseas and domestic divisions. Sly's powers of persuasion worked a unanimous "yes" of support out of staff after a three-day meeting. In January of 1968, Kenneth A. Kuntz, the retired Wickizer's successor, laid out structure changes for the domestic division, now called the Division of Homeland Ministries. Thomas J. Liggett succeeded Sly upon his retirement October 1, 1968, just as restructure was approved. Liggett carried out the UCMS restructuring, serving as deputy general minister and president in the restructured church as well.

In 1969 the UCMS abolished its board of managers and initiated procedures that would have the General Assembly of the church elect its directors. On January 1, 1971, it released its two major divisions to the whole church as the separate "provisional" Divisions of Homeland Ministries and Overseas Ministries, each with its own program board. The divisions incorporated separately April 1, 1973. At the same time the UCMS transferred its 222 South Downey Avenue building management staff to a subsidiary organization of the General Assembly and settled back, with one employee, to continue existence only as a foundation, managing permanent funds received over the years and dividing the earnings between the two divisions.

Other Developments

The National Benevolent Association, another of the larger recipients of the church's outreach funds, at the time of restructure was serving 2,000 people annually through eight children's homes and eleven homes for the aged. Church offerings represented about 25 percent of NBA's operating budget, the remainder coming from resident fees, permanent fund earnings, and gifts from individuals and groups. On May 5, 1970, NBA's board voted to accept the role of Division of Social and Health Services for the restructured church, though legal and promotional considerations stood in the way of a name change.

NBA services expanded enormously over the next 15 years primarily because of government-funded programs of care and housing for the aging. NBA also expanded its efforts in serving retarded individuals, emotionally and physically handicapped and began research into such areas as Alzheimer's disease, funded by a non-church grant. By 1985 NBA either owned, operated or managed 58 centers of social or health services with 7,000 persons in residence. Since the growth of church offerings during the period was slow and costs of social and health care had ballooned, the percentage of NBA's operating budget of $44 million covered by church offerings fell to less than six percent by the mid-1980s.

The Pension Fund was typical of the agencies that felt obligated to protect their funds in relating to the restructured church. The Fund leaders affirmed their desire to be an active part of the church and its work. The Fund changed its name to the Pension Fund of the Christian Church (Disciples of Christ)—from Pension Fund of Christian Churches—and indicated its willingness to enter an interim arrangement, with the right to agree or not agree once a constitution for the Disciples was prepared. The caution expressed by the board was protecting its legal, financial, contractual and actuarial obligations.

Nevertheless, the Pension Fund submitted its audit and actuarial reports to the plenary bodies of the church regularly in addition to the service reports. It participated fully in Church Finance Council promotional efforts, received allocations through the Commission on Finance, revised the Pension Plan and inaugurated a new comprehensive health care plan for ministers and church employees through resolutions to the General Assembly, sent its president to the General Cabinet and Council of Ministers, and consulted the general minister and president when searching for a new president of its own.

Pension Fund President Lester D. Palmer, looking back over the years, noted in 1986: "Some of the fears and apprehensions of those early days of the restructuring process were no doubt justified. The board members, at the time, could not visualize the covenantal relationship that now exists. They were intent on protecting the contractual relationships that exist with Pension Plan members and beneficiaries and were frightened at the prospect of 'control' from outside. Fiduciary responsibility is still uppermost in the mind of Pension Fund board members but the experience of the past 18 years has proven that the church values such responsibility and does not want to impinge upon it. The Pension Fund, as a general administrative unit described in the Design, has been free to administer its program and financial affairs within the limits of its Articles of Incorporation and Bylaws. Mutual consent and the integrity of this organization have been maintained."

Creating a Foundation

One of the fruits of restructure was the Christian Church Foundation, the unit of the church at the general level that deals with large individual gifts and long-term gifts to underwrite church cause. Prior to restructure, the Foundation was an arm of Unified Promotion (Church Finance Council). A task force chaired by Harry T. Ice, Indianapolis attorney considered one of that city's "movers and shakers," recommended in 1967 that the Foundation be spun off as a separate unit, and at the 1969 General Assembly it was, under President James R. Reed. At that time the Foundation's assets were $169,000. At the end of 1985 the assets exceeded $20 million. Earnings on the Foundation's holdings are distributed among the outreach arms of the church on the same percentage as Basic Mission Finance.

Though Disciples of Christ endowments hardly matched those of most other major American church bodies, there were achievements in philanthropy. Those who had given long-term gifts to the United Christian Missionary Society made it possible for the successor Divisions of Homeland and Overseas Ministries to carry out much of their work with minimal administration costs.

Of the many philanthropists of the church, Theodore P. Beasley, founder of Republic National Life Insurance, stands out. The Dallas man's gifts to Texas Christian University, Phillips University and Lexington Theological Seminary, to Juliette Fowler homes, his underwriting of the Foundation, his assisting with buildings for the Division of Higher Education-NBA in St. Louis and for National City Christian Church in Washington, D.C., and his planning grant for a new Disciples of Christ headquarters building in Indianapolis totaled more than $22 million.

Changes in the Funding Process

The Finance Council envisioned under restructure did not come into being until July 1, 1974. It differed from its predecessor,

Unified Promotion, in that it was the financial arm of the church, not a creature of participating agencies. Where Unified Promotion was governed by a board of 78 representatives—one from each of the agencies, the Church Finance Council had a board of 31 representatives of the "church." Where Unified Promotion's ultimate loyalties were to the agencies that had banded together to promote funds, Church Finance Council was subject to the stewardship policies of the General Assembly of the church.

The basic outreach funding process was changed significantly with the coming of the Finance Council. There was disagreement over whether it was an improvement. For the most part, general unit executives believed that it was not an improvement since the portion of Basic Mission Finance going to general work of the church steadily declined while the portion to the regions increased. Under the pre-Finance Council arrangement, all organizations of the church—states and areas and institutions as well as general agencies—received binding allocations from an impartial commission. Under the new plan, the regional allocations were only "recommendations" and could be negotiated. When the regions negotiated larger shares, the total outreach pool for the general manifestation was reduced. The net effect was that in 15 years the regions were receiving 36 percent of all outreach as opposed to 29 percent. Some regions argued that it made sense that regional operations should have the first option on funds originating in their regions. Others called attention to the increasing need for regional programming as part of the "megatrend" in society toward decentralization. General units argued that the church concept agreed to by all parties was equal manifestations, not a pyramid either of authority or funding.

Funding questions and the concept of covenant spurred a new relationship in the mid-1970s between the church and its higher education institutions.

Harlie L. Smith had said at the outset of restructure on October 2, 1962: "The church without the college and its learning can become dogmatic, sterile, irrelevant and given only to emotional sentimentality. The college without the church and her faith can lose its purpose and soul and become so coldly intellectual that it will engage in only meaningless intellectual exercise in the atmosphere of a deep freeze." Today there are 18 church-related colleges and universities, plus four seminaries and three divinity houses serving, in total, more than 22,000 students from 47 states and 28 foreign countries.

In the first General Board meeting eight months after restructure was adopted, a comprehensive study on ministerial education was authorized. That study, under the direction of the Board of Higher Education, was published in 1973 and entitled The Imperative is Leadership. In response to the study, the 1975 General Assembly in San Antonio commended development of a coordinating entity to embrace the concerns of the professional ministry. The Assembly also called for an evaluation of seminary education and such a study was authorized by the Administrative Committee in 1977. The question was: Did the Disciples need seven theological education institutions? The answer after a year of study was "yes."

The church set in place a Higher Education Evaluation Task Force in 1975 to work the next year toward a funding solution for the colleges. In 1976 the Task Force recommended the development of a covenantal relationship between the church and its related colleges and universities that placed the funding of the liberal arts institutions in the context of a church investment in ministry. The covenantal relationship did not really increase the Disciples' financial allocation to higher education but it brought a more equitable distribution of the money that was available.

The covenant committed the church to distribute to each undergraduate institution a base amount of $30,000 per year, $10 additional for each full-time equivalent undergraduate student, $100 for each full-time equivalent undergraduate Disciples of Christ student, and $500 for each graduate enrolling in an accredited seminary. Further, the covenant arrangement called upon the church to help secure donors for the institutions, recruit students for them, and act as a learning and research testing ground for the colleges and universities. In return, the institutions were expected to reflect the Judeo-Christian tradition, provide opportunity for biblical studies, share personnel with the church and offer opportunity for the spiritual development of students.

The institutions began to sign the covenant individually in late 1977 opening a new era of relationship to the Christian Church (Disciples of Christ). The new era also was marked by a change from the Board of Higher Education to a Division of Higher Education—funded by the church rather than by institutional dues. Called to the position of president of the new division was a layman, D. Duane Cummins, professor of history at Oklahoma City University.

Missouri Challenges System

The higher education institutions in the Missouri (now Mid-America) region were involved in the first challenge to the basic fund allocations process of the restructured church. The Missouri regional board decided in April, 1975 that the region would begin collecting the outreach contributions of Missouri congregations direct if that state's higher education institutions did not receive the full amounts requested from Basic Mission Finance. Four of the schools had objected to their 1974 allocations. This pullout from Church Finance Council was averted only after intensive negotiation and a July 15, 1975, agreement between Spencer P. Austin, president of the Church Finance Council, and Lester B. Rickman, Missouri regional minister, in which there was a compromise, the gist of which was that the Finance Council would distribute the amount the institutions wanted for the next two years, the region would play by the rules thereafter, and the extra money would be raised with a special promotional effort.

Also in 1975, the region of Ohio tried to ease the financial woes of theological education through General Assembly action. Ohio filed a resolution that would have established a Seminary Fund from congregational offerings with one percent of congregational budgets earmarked for the seminaries. The Assembly rejected the resolution because a designated fund would undercut the principle upon which Disciples funding was based—the principle that mission beyond the congregation was strongest when money remained undesignated and could be applied to world needs as circumstances and reasoned evaluation dictated.

A Churchwide Financial Campaign

There was a great deal of enthusiasm in 1971 for a Churchwide Financial Campaign which would be conducted during the second quadrennium of the newly restructured church, 1975-79. However, a feasibility study brought the proposed campaign's steering committee to conclude in 1975: "Members of the Christian Church, including many key leaders, are not at present prepared to provide the type of support required for an effective churchwide financial campaign." The church's Administrative Committee set in motion studies which suggested what the Disciples needed instead was an improved program of fund development through regular processes. The 1975 General Assembly supported that. The effort would be to raise the level of giving of congregations for all purposes, provide strengthened estate planning and deferred giving services, and to cultivate and solicit special gifts. On the long-term and special gift side of that there were beginnings in the 1980s of annual consultation between development officers. Intentions were expressed by some development officers to raise money for the church at large rather than only the units for which they work.

The Tough Question of Planning

After the restructure vote the church took on the task of program planning and priorities. The 1971 General Assembly in Louisville adopted a statement relative to "the process of developing the work" of the Christian Church. In that statement it was acknowledged that the planning councils, inter-agency committees and various forms of inter-board cooperation had helped bring the "sense of church" to Disciples that led to restructure. The Louisville statement gave executive responsibility for general unit planning to the General Minister and President and the GMP's cabinet with responsibility for overall planning to the Council of Ministers (which included both General Cabinet and regional ministers). Planning in the mid-1980s still lacked adequate congregational participation, and much planning continued being done in isolation among general units and regions.

The first biennial Assembly in Seattle in 1969 adopted what were called "mission imperatives" that served as the basis for the first set of priorities under the new quadrennial planning process. The 1971 Assembly followed up its action on the planning statement by adopting five priorities plus an "enabling imperative"—finance. The five were: evangelism and renewal; leadership; ecumenical involvement; reconciliation in the urban crisis; and world order, justice and peace.

Few people objected to the list. The major problem was that practically all present efforts of the church fit somewhere into one of the categories. Also, there was no funding for the denominational priorities unless units and regions of the church shifted it within their own budgets. That was difficult because finance had come into hard times. In 1970, the offerings for outreach had declined for the first time by 2.6 percent after averaging gains of 3.3 percent the previous five years. The loss was even greater—3.5 percent—in 1971 but recovery was strong with 8.3 percent gains each of the next two years. Nevertheless, as inflation skyrocketed, Disciples had to deal with an upcoming decade in which cost-of-living regularly outpaced income increases, resulting in a struggle to keep current program intact, with little thought to new program or switching budgets to meet denominational priorities.

On the basis of the recommendations of a task force appointed by the General Minister and President, the five-fold priority of the 1971-75 period was extended two years through 1977. In 1977 the priorities were narrowed to two: Reach out globally to alleviate hunger and extend human rights, and renew congregational life and witness. They were readopted in 1981 with the addition of a third. Kenneth Teegarden made a special appeal at the 1981 Assembly in Anaheim on behalf of a peace priority and "Pursue peace with justice" was added for the quadrennium through 1985 "with the concern for peace taking a special emphasis within the whole." In Des Moines in 1985 the three were extended for another two years.

Who Speaks for the Church?

As the General Board of the restructured church struggled to see precisely what its role was, an issue emerged that helped the church focus on that role. In St. Louis' Jefferson Hotel June 12, 1972, the board faced a resolution calling upon the United States to end its trade embargo against communist Cuba. William J. Nottingham, then Latin America secretary, spoke strongly in favor, objecting to the innumerable hardships of the embargo on the Cuban people. The question was raised, however, by Peoria attorney Randall A. West, immediate past Vice Moderator, whether the General Board could speak on such an issue when the *Provisional Design* gives the board only the right to take interim action "within established policy" of the General Assembly.

"If we vote this recommended action," West told the board, "we are expanding and upgrading the authority of the General Board to make policy statements in behalf of the Christian

Church." He felt that such action was not within the letter and the spirit of the governing document of the restructured church. Despite a need for timely action, West argued, such action would bring increased pressure on the board to take actions without waiting for the more representative General Assembly which meets only every two years. West said that if it is proper for general units of the church to bring to the board items for immediate action, it should also be proper for congregations to do likewise.

The General Board decided to take its chances, speak its best mind subject to censure by the Assembly and to take to the Cincinnati Assembly an action clarifying its role in witnessing in its own name. When General Assembly arrived in 1973, however, the larger body voted down the proposal that the General Board be permitted to adopt resolutions in its own name between Assemblies. The Assembly feeling was that the church's public witness—or at least the policy on which it is based—ought to remain in the hands of the largest representative body of Disciples.

West took pains to make certain the General Board hearkened to the Assembly's decision. At the June, 1974, meeting of the General Board, he questioned again whether the board had authority to speak on a matter involving housing subsidies for low income persons.

Adopting a Symbol

An indication of the need of Disciples of Christ for some publicly recognizable tie to each other was the rapid spread of the symbol—the red chalice bearing the X-shaped cross of St. Andrew. Even before the symbol of the restructured church was officially adopted, it was appearing everywhere—on business cards, stationery, newsletters, on churches overseas, in stained glass, on street signs. It was even on an Independent Christian Church in Lexington, Kentucky (until the church was advised what it represented!)

The hockey team sponsored by the Princess Avenue Disciples of Christ Church in St. Thomas, Ontario, sailed across the ice in snow-white uniforms with that flaming red chalice on the front, St. Andrew's cross and all.

One of the blessings many Disciples saw in a restructured

church was that they would be more readily identified in public. The Administrative Committee authorized the Office of Communication to use the symbol on a "trial basis" in early 1970. The General Assembly adopted it 20 months later. By then it would have taken intervention by divine authority to have halted its spread.

The symbol had an explanation that was logical. St. Andrew was the patron saint of Scotland and the Disciples forebears came out of Scottish Presbyterianism. Alexander Campbell studied in Glasgow. The free church ideas that the Campbells brought with them to North America had their origins in Scotland. Then there was the tradition of the Apostle Andrew. He brought his brother Peter to Christ. Andrew appealed to Disciples. He was evangelistic. The X-shaped cross became the symbol of St. Andrew because of the tradition that Andrew had requested one, feeling he was not worthy to be crucified as Christ was.

The Disciples symbol was first drawn—much as it appears now—in Indianapolis early in 1970 on a restaurant napkin! The person who sketched it was Ronald Osborn. He was fed ideas by the director of the church's Office of Communication, Robert L. Friedly. The two had been asked by a small committee chaired by Osborn to come up with something quickly since the committee had rejected more than 200 designs suggested by Disciples from throughout North America. Friedly had seen the St. Andrew's cross among the "Symbols of Our Faith" on a denominational worship bulletin March 31, 1968, and was intrigued with the potential of tying it to Disciples. The final rendering was done by commercial artist Bruce Tilsley of Denver, Colorado. Tilsley offered half a dozen alternatives—probably more artistic—but the two Indianapolis men insisted on the napkin version.

The 1971 General Assembly adopted a resolution approving the Chalice-and-St. Andrew's Cross as the "official symbol" of the Christian Church (Disciples of Christ). It did so in light of the "widespread acceptance and use of this symbol." There was discussion from the floor, largely expressing a lack of appreciation for the St. Andrew's Cross as opposed to the more traditional cross of Christ. Connie Purser of Eminence, Kentucky, urged that the chalice be tipped as if it were pouring out God's love to all; that way, in addition, the cross would be upright, looking more traditional. Her suggestions were heard in good spirit by the

Assembly. But there was no action to incorporate them in the motion.

* * *

"Stories of . . . exemplary individuals are an important part of the tradition that is so central to a community of memory."

IRMA DIAZ loves young people, or jovenes in the Spanish language. A social case worker in Brooklyn, she heard God's call, twice, in this lay ministry. The first was in native Puerto Rico. The second was in 1967 in Brooklyn. She had been in the United States with her mother for seven years. But she was wondering if in fact her mission was not back in Puerto Rico. Mother was happy on the mainland; she had two sons who lived in New York. There would be a separation if Irma went back.

Decision time had come and it was a tearful moment. Suddenly there was a knock at the door. A woman was standing there, a woman unknown to Irma Diaz or her mother. She had a large Bible in her hand, and she said: "I was praying in my house, and the word came to me that there was a crisis here, and that I should come and pray with you."

They let her in and Diaz still does not know the woman's name or where she came from, but they knelt together and prayed. God spoke to her clearly in that moment, Diaz remembers. "I know you are suffering and I am with you. I told you I had a ministry for you." Irma Diaz has been in Brooklyn ever since. Her mother died the following year. As the youngest in the family, she felt she must follow her mother's devotion and serve the church. It was God's plan. She had a mission.

Diaz was a co-founder of the Confraternidad de Jovenes of the Hispanic Disciples of Christ congregations, of which there were eleven, in the Northeastern Region of the United States. Over the years she has worked with hundreds of young people who have grown up to become leaders in the church. She organized La Tamborina in Sinai Christian Church—a group of sin-ger-musicians that perform widely in churches and for the City of New York volunteer services in places ranging from homes for the elderly to prisons. The group is accompanied by tamborines, piano, saxophone and drums. With money they sometimes received for their services La Tamborina bought gifts for the people to whom they sang.

Diaz has supervised youth on countless conferences and retreats. She was the first woman to chair a board of any of the Hispanic congregations in the Northeastern area. She was the first woman vice-president of La Junta, the Hispanic Northeastern convention. She represented the young people at the outset of the national Hispanic Fellowship junta as it organized in the mid-1970s.

"I just love young people," says Irma Diaz as she feeds her dogs in her Williamsburg section co-op. "When I was growing up I wish that someone had gotten real interested in me. I didn't have a father. My mother was widowed when she was very young. I had a lot of questions. I went through a lot of spiritual questioning. Spiritual retreats helped me a lot. But I wish I had someone who would listen to me. My minister was very old. A lot of people kept telling me you can't do this, and don't do that.

"When I see the young people in my church, they're like I was. And I say to myself, 'The Lord gave you that ministry.' It is hard to deal with them sometimes. They want things their way. People in the church get very confused. They are always surrounded with young people. Young people want you to listen to them. To understand."

Irma Diaz grew up in the town of Cataño, which she remembers as being about a 10-minute boat ride from the capital of San Juan. She spent her high school years in Cataño and attended a couple of summers at the University of Puerto Rico. She felt that God spoke to her about ministry before she ever left the island. She became a literacy teacher. Her mother came to the United States with grandson Roberto in 1960 and Irma, selling all the family possessions, followed nine months later.

Diaz was unaware of the Sinai church and she attended various churches including La Hermosa Christian Church in Manhattan. Finally, someone told her that there was a Hispanic Disciples of Christ congregation near where she lived, one called Sinai. She knew "as soon as I entered the door, it was for me." Still a teenager herself, Diaz organized a youth class of 12 to 14-year-olds which quickly quadrupled in size from the original 10. Only three months after her arrival at Sinai she was elected president of the youth society.

She took a job with the New York City social services operation as an income maintenance specialist. She held the position almost 20 years before becoming a social case worker. In 1986, Irma Diaz completed her bachelor of science degree in sociology at Boricua College, a bilingual institution in Brooklyn.

She was described by Juan Rodriguez of Hammond, Indiana, president of the National Hispanic and Bilingual Fellowship, as a dynamic lay leader of Hispanic Disciples of Christ. Her youth organization, he said, has "produced leadership for our local congregations, fostered unity, led young persons to professional ministry." Diaz is not sure of the number of her youth who have gone into ministry but the list includes pastors, music ministers, and at least one missionary and one chaplain. She says: "It is beautiful to see young people answer God's call!"

6

Discovering Diversity

1969—*Nixon inaugurated* (Jan. 20) . . . *U.S. Vietnam forces peak at 543,400* (April) . . . Disciples/Roman Catholic talks begin . . . General Board responds to Black Manifesto (May 27) . . . *Kennedy involved at Chappaquiddick* (July 18) . . . *Armstrong walks on moon* (July 20) . . . First Assembly at Seattle doubles race, poverty commitment to $4 million (Aug. 15-20) . . . *Massive Vietnam protests* (Oct. 15) . . . *My Lai massacre uncovered* (Nov. 16) . . . Consultations held on merging CWF, CMF into laity department.

1970—*Miners' Yablonski murdered* (Jan. 5) . . . *Biafra surrenders to Nigeria* (Jan. 12) . . . Beazley elected chair of COCU (March 13) . . . *First Earth Day* (April 22) . . . *4 killed at Kent State* (May 4) . . . 3,500 women at Quadrennial (June 22-26) . . . *Independent U.S. postal service created* (Aug. 12) . . . First Black Convocation in Columbia, Mo. (August 19-23) . . . World Convention, Adelaide, Australia.

Black militant James Foreman burst upon the American religious scene in a singularly dramatic way in 1969 and disappeared almost as quickly. While bedeviling a number of church denominations by disrupting Sunday worship with demands for millions of dollars in "reparations" for past injustices to blacks, he ignored the Disciples of Christ. But the Disciples could not ignore him. Their General Board convened only weeks after Foreman's advent, the first national board of any denomination to do so. The nation's ear was poised to hear how churches would respond to the "Black Manifesto."

The General Board's 4,500-word message resulting from the Black Manifesto is one of the denomination's most important documents in the quarter century. The James Foreman episode had several effects on the Disciples: (1) It shocked many basically well-meaning Disciples out of their insensitivity to the church's role in racial oppression and the need to rectify it; (2) it made racial inclusiveness a part of future Disciples conversation about elections, appointments, hirings, recruitment; (3) it gave the one

85

out of every twenty Disciples who are black, Hispanic or American Asian new visibility and helped make Disciples aware they do have an ethnic constituency; and, (4) it nudged the church to employ, elect and appoint ethnic persons, the results surprising many white Disciples with the number of quality ethnic leaders in the church and establishing that leadership as a permanent factor in the Disciples' life.

The response to the Manifesto put the church's "Reconciliation" race and poverty program into church life on a permanent basis as a special offering alongside the Week of Compassion, the relief and development program that is oriented overseas. Reconciliation had its roots in the Committee on Moral and Civil Rights appointed by Disciples about two months before King's "I Have a Dream" speech in 1963.

The committee sent tons of food to Mississippi to blacks who lost their jobs because of civil rights activity, involved more than 2,000 ministers in rights ministries, helped relocate several southern ministers who got into difficulty because of their civil rights connections, provided a full-time staff couple for the National Council of Churches in Mississippi voter registration and community organization in 1964 and 1965, offered a base of operations for the National Council's Delta Ministry at the former Southern Christian Institute property in Edwards, Mississippi, and raised $168,000 through mid-1967 in support of the effort. Some 100 to 150 Disciples were involved in activities on the scene of the Selma-Montgomery march, including A. Dale Fiers and Mae Yoho Ward, executive of the International Convention and vice-president of the United Christian Missionary Society respectively.

By 1967, with the riots in ghettos in the cities, the focus of the rights movement turned to the urban situation. The International Convention took action that year calling for response by Disciples. In mid-1968 the International Convention appointed a five-member steering committee to give overall direction to the urban issue. One of the committee members was John R. Compton, the black associate secretary of the Ohio Society of Christian Churches, who was to become one of the major racial ground breakers in the church's life.

In March of 1968, Compton accepted the job in Indianapolis of staff director of "Reconciliation: The Urban Emergency Program of the Christian Churches." It was just a few days prior to the assassination of Martin Luther King Jr. Twenty-five days after the assassination the Disciples held a special consultation on urban emergency strategy to see what the role of the church should be in dealing with the problems that led to ghetto rioting the past three years. Reconciliation immediately launched a $2 million-plus campaign through mid-1970. To get the program off the ground at once, $116,000 was loaned to Reconciliation, including $50,000 each by the Board of Church Extension and the United Christian Missionary Society.

Drafting A Manifesto Response

Unintentionally, James Foreman helped inaugurate Reconciliation in a big way. The Disciples response to the Manifesto doubled the church's Reconciliation commitment to $4 million. The Manifesto response, drafted during the May 24-27 General Board meeting in St. Louis in 1969, was the work of vice-moderator Albert M. Pennybacker, 36-year-old activist pastor from Shaker Heights, Ohio, of Compton, and of Ronald Osborn. The three of them ate breakfast together at Pope's Cafeteria on Sunday morning, deciding that Osborn would write a section conveying a message from the General Board to the church, that Compton would write proposals for action and Pennybacker guidelines for congregations. Osborn skipped morning worship and the afternoon section meeting, pounding away on a typewriter in the press room.

That night the executive committee took a look at the work of the three and Moderator James M. Moudy concluded, "This is a remarkable document." Debate in the committee centered on specific proposals for action. Frank G. Reid, a Chicago pastor, dramatized the desperation of blacks: "A prisoner counts his days."

Pennybacker put the writing into a single document that night and he, Compton and Osborn met again for breakfast the next morning. At the General Board session that morning Pennybacker read the message and was greeted by applause. Then, following floor debate, the three, "weary to the point of grogginess" Osborn recalls, worked on revisions until 7:45 p.m. The next morning the response was overwhelmingly adopted. The result was a document that other denominations used as a model.

Essentially, it denounced racism (including black racism), confessed the timidity of the church in dealing with racism, rejected violence and separatism (including white separatism), rejected extortion and revenge, and called upon the church to stop "business as usual" and seek reconciliation in a time of urgent crisis.

On May 26 when the response to the Manifesto was brought to the floor for initial discussion KMOX television set up equipment to film. That resulted in an attempt to close the board meeting to the press, some leaders feeling that the glare of publicity might hinder open discussion or subject congregations to controversy, and perhaps even violence. Again Ronald Osborn provided some of the conclusive wisdom. He slipped a note to those fighting to keep the meeting open, saying that the church is an open society and should not be afraid to debate its decisions publicly, "even when subject to distortion!"

In his diary at the end of the day, Osborn wrote: "Once in five years the church does something of public interest, then gets nervous about it!" The General Board stayed open and there were no other attempts in the next 15 years of the restructured church to close plenary gatherings. Further, the boards of the Divisions of Homeland and Overseas Ministries took actions to declare their own board meetings open to press and constituency, within the limitations only of space.

20 Percent Ethnic Representation

In August, the General Assembly overwhelmingly approved the response to the Black Manifesto. Of the actions called for, one that quickly became imbedded in policy was a goal of 20 percent of staffs and boards of the church being ethnic minority persons. Compton originally suggested the figure—as the document said— "to symbolize the commitment we have to a raceless community." Racism never would be dealt with until there was sufficient contact between the races to permit "constructive interaction."

The 20 percent figure was drawn out of the air by Compton— a "moon shot," one from which he could compromise downward if necessary. The minority constituency of the church was only five percent. But, in what many Disciples would see as one of those interventions by the Holy Spirit, the figure stuck. The minority presence, in larger than token numbers, added a richness and dynamic edge to the church's work and deliberations that it would never have had otherwise.

Shortly, the General Board and the Administrative Committee of the church reflected the 20 percent commitment in their makeup. The complexions of unit and regional boards began to change in that direction as well. Professional staffs changed too. For instance, in 1985 the Division of Homeland Ministries, with the largest of the general unit executive staffs at 38, had an ethnic minority ratio of 26 percent—more than double what it was two decades earlier. Overseas Ministries, in the same period, went from zero to 23 percent in black, Hispanic and American Asian executives. Many units moved more slowly but there was change, and constant pressure.

John Compton was a remarkable individual. Quiet and unassuming, but able to exert considerable pressure behind the scenes, he had served on the boards of the International Convention and UCMS when black visibility was extremely low in the positions of power among the Disciples. For 17 years a pastor in Cincinnati, he had marched with Martin Luther King Jr. in the south and associated with the civil rights leader in working on Cleveland, Ohio's problems while Compton was associate executive on the Disciples' Ohio staff.

While Compton was at the Dallas convention in 1966 racists burned his home in a white Cleveland suburb. He coped in that personal tragedy with humor, remarking in 1970 to A. Dale Fiers as the Disciples executive welcomed him to a position in Indianapolis with the suggestion he have a house-warming: "No thanks. Had one of those!"

Able to function within both white and black societies while retaining the trust and confidence of both, Compton established a number of firsts for minority persons in the Disciples. He was the first black staff attached full-time to the chief executive of the church. He was the first black to become a regional minister of the church (Indiana in 1979). He was the first black president of a major division of the church (Division of Homeland Ministries, beginning in 1982).

Black Disciples in History

The year 1969 was the year in which terms of a merger were worked out between the black National Christian Missionary

Convention and the white structures. Blacks had identified with the Disciples of Christ from the movement's beginnings on the frontier. Many in North Carolina had Baptist origins. The church's second missionary in 1853 was a black, Alexander Cross. He went to Liberia and died there two years later. The black Southern Christian Institute in Mississippi and Jarvis Christian College in Texas produced excellent leaders. But just as the blacks at the old Cane Ridge Meeting House were forced to go in via ladder and sit in the balcony, participation always was on the fringe, largely because whites did not really see blacks as equals.

Preston Taylor, in Memphis in 1917, organized the National Christian Missionary Convention, with the realization that blacks were not going to get appropriate opportunities for leadership in the white church structures. Emmett Dickson, a teacher at Jarvis, came to Indianapolis to serve as full-time staff of the black Convention after World War II. He worked with black women's groups and other black structures in 14 states, 11 of which still had segregated state convention organizations. The black Disciples had separate leadership development, church development and other programs but, by agreement, those were merged into the UCMS in 1960 and Dickson became director of church relations on the UCMS staff, still working largely with the black Disciples.

That merger of program took place under the leadership of Compton and William K. Fox, presidents of the National Christian Missionary Convention during the period. Even then there was an eye toward merging the business of the black Disciples with the International Convention, which had no segregation policy and where it would be front and center for all church members, inspirational to blacks, educational for whites. That happened in 1970 with Raymond E. Brown, Compton's stepbrother, in the leadership role. The structure brought black and white action and business together, while leaving a new every-other-year meeting called the National Convocation of the Christian Church as something of a caucus organization of black Disciples, as well as a fellowship and black church training event.

Blacks began to emerge in traditional leadership positions for the whole church in the late 1950s. Compton was elected to the board of the International Convention in 1957, where he served for six years. He began serving on the UCMS board as well in

1960. Mrs. R. H. Peoples, an Indianapolis pastor's wife, served as International Convention vice-president in 1959. Mrs. Carnella Barnes of Los Angeles was vice-president in 1962. She also was to become the first black president of the International Christian Women's Fellowship. S. S. Myers, Kansas City pastor, was elected a vice-president of the convention in 1966 and blacks have had a position in the top three elected offices ever since.

Walter D. Bingham, a Louisville pastor, became the first black Moderator of the church in 1971 and led the denomination's first fraternal visit to the churches of Asia the following year. Raymond E. Brown joined the staff of the Board of Church Extension as general consultant in 1970 and became one of the most powerful blacks in church leadership. He became senior vice-president of the Board by 1981, where he made major decisions about millions of dollars in loans to churches building or remodeling facilities. He also played a role in the Board's program of interest-free loans to ethnic and newly-organized churches.

Concerns of Black Disciples

The National Convocation in 1971 brought to the floor of the General Assembly a series of concerns about the church, the nation and black Disciples. The concerns included low wages of black pastors, the need for new black congregations, more relevant program materials, improved communication, continuing education and black ministerial recruitment, ministerial employment, support of Jarvis Christian College, a Martin Luther King holiday, reduction of military expenses and a withdrawal from Vietnam where "blacks are bearing more than their share of the casualties."

It was a formidable list, enumerating what black Disciples were thinking as they gave up their own convention for fuller involvement in the General Assembly. But it also was a demonstration that the minority constituency wanted inclusion in the General Assembly processes to be real, not sham. The list resulted in the establishment of the Office of Black Ministry in the Division of Homeland Ministries. Among the recommendations was one urging significant attention be given to the development of black churches. That idea was picked up in the 1980s in a major new church establishment program called "Church Advance Now." That program called for the establishment of 100 new congregations during the 1980s, 30 percent of them being ethnic—15 percent black, 10 percent Hispanic and five percent Asian. The office of the General Minister and President assisted in the production of a black periodical called *Update*. The church did declare a King holiday for most general staff and worked for the adoption of the federal holiday. It also continued to press for an end to the Vietnam conflict.

The program to meet the urban emergency was made a permanent part of the Disciples' over-and-above offering soon after the Manifesto response. The offering became an annual one in September and October. Each year it raised about a half-million dollars for programs of jobs, housing, white-racism education, and other race and poverty needs. Reconciliation continued throughout the remaining years of the Restructure era and became an equal—in importance, if not in dollars—to the Disciples' relief and development offering, Week of Compassion.

Black sensitivities to oppressive treatment resulted in a 1972 confrontation in General Board that ended in the Disciples rescinding a decision to hold the 1975 General Assembly in Salt Lake City. Utah had only three churches and had sought the General Assembly as a means of witnessing to the larger community, one dominated by the Church of Jesus Christ of Latter Day Saints. The board voted in favor of holding the Assembly in Salt Lake City. But after the vote black members raised the question of discrimination against blacks by the Mormons. They questioned whether the Disciples should feed an economy controlled by Mormons. Andrew W. Ramsey, an Indianapolis layman, asserted that he could get discriminated against for free at home, why should he go to Salt Lake City and pay for it?

The General Board rescinded its action and instructed staff to arrange the Assembly either in Denver or San Antonio instead. The board told the General Minister and President to communicate "in love" the reasons for the change to Salt Lake City authorities and the Mormon church. The tiny Disciples community in Utah was deeply disappointed. The action prompted the Church of Jesus Christ of Latter Day Saints to send to Indianapolis two men to explain the position of the church with respect to blacks.

The meeting was cordial and no attempt was made to have Disciples change their minds about the assembly location. One of the visiting Mormons was black and he explained to Disciples leaders that while the Mormons did not, at the present, permit blacks in the priesthood, the elders had revelations from time to time that changed basic policies in the church.

A few years later the Church of Jesus Christ of Latter Day Saints had just such a revelation and opened the door to blacks in the priesthood. Disciples who remembered the encounter wondered if perhaps the Disciples' vote might not have been a factor in preparing for the revelation.

The Hispanic Presence

While the black constituency of the Disciples of Christ has been estimated by black Disciples at 50,000 persons in nearly 500 predominantly black congregations, there is a growing Hispanic presence in some 35 largely Hispanic or bilingual congregations, in addition to those Hispanic persons affiliated with non-Hispanic congregations. Hispanics had their first congregational identity among the Disciples of Christ in San Antonio in 1899.

Hispanics, like blacks, have not become a part of the American cultural melting pot. David A. Vargas, Latin American executive for the Disciples in the mid-1980s, believed that the continued separation may be related to the geographic proximity of Latin America, voluntary and involuntary segregation, and the victimization of prejudice.

A few Hispanics were involved in church leadership in the early 1960s, but only a few. Apolonio Melecio, pastor of the famed La Hermosa (The Beautiful) Christian Church in New York City, served on the International Convention board of directors. Michael Saenz, a Laredo, Texas, native who earned a Ph.D. degree in business administration from the University of Pennsylvania, helped the Disciples of Puerto Rico organize their convention, then returned to the United States convinced that the island Disciples no longer needed missionary assistance.

He worked for several years as the manager of Disciples headquarters facilities in Indianapolis before heading back to Texas, where he became president of the one of the community colleges in the Tarrant County system at Fort Worth. Pablo Cotto helped establish Hispanic work in New York and Texas, then served for a time in the 1970s as a Disciples' missionary in Argentina.

93

Origins of a national Disciples organization by Hispanics date to 1970-71 although Texas Hispanics date their state work back to 1916. Disciples chronicle their relationship to the historic Mexican Christian Institute in San Antonio, now Inman Christian Center, back to the same period. The Rev. Doroteo Alaniz notes that there was a "State Mexican S.S. Convention" in Texas in 1916 involving two congregations in Mexico, one in San Antonio, one in Sabinas, one in Lockhart and one in Robstown. The Northeast Convention of Hispanic Churches was organized in 1958 in the Bronx. Twenty years later the Midwest Hispanic and Bilingual Convention came into existence in Gary, Indiana, with congregations represented from Gary, Chicago, Lorain (Ohio) and Kansas City.

During the 1960s a major effort was made to increase awareness of Hispanics among Disciples. The United Christian Missionary Society published a book called *Six Million Americans* in 1964. Byron Spice, who had been a Latin America missionary, headed up homeland missions for a part of the time and is credited with much of the work toward awareness among Disciples of the Hispanic element in the church.

Domingo Rodriquez in 1969 became the first Hispanic director of program services on the staff of Homeland Missions. A book about Hispanics, *Dignidad*, became a part of the curriculum of the church in 1975. It was authored by Lucas Torres, a successor to Rodriguez. By that time the estimate of Americans with an Hispanic heritage had reached 14 million.

The roots of the national Hispanic organization can be found in a gathering April 6-10, 1970. It was the first conference of Hispanic American ministers. The site was Indianapolis, under the impetus of the United Christian Missionary Society and with thirty-eight ministers from 11 states, Puerto Rico and Mexico participating. A committee out of that conference produced four recommendations: (1) a permanent conference of Hispanic American ministers be established, with financial assistance from the general church; (2) scholarships for Hispanic ministerial candidates be established; (3) Spanish language Christian education materials be developed; and (4) Hispanics be allowed to elect their own representatives to the General Board and Administrative Committee of the church. Though the objectives never were fully met, the national organization had been initiated.

Hispanic ministers continued to meet, adding lay representatives to their gatherings in the mid-1970s. The committee that had been organized by the Office of the General Minister and President and had related exclusively to blacks prior to 1976 became the Committee on Black and Hispanic Concerns (now the Committee on Racial Ethnic Inclusiveness and Empowerment). Eight black and eight Hispanic members, along with leaders of general units of the church, began to meet regularly in December to deal with ethnic issues.

The Hispanic caucus of that committee generated the idea for a National Hispanic and Bilingual Fellowship and accompanying assembly. The first Hispanic assembly took place in Indianapolis June 24-26, 1981. More than 300 persons from 24 Hispanic congregations in the Southwest, Midwest and Northeast "juntas" and from church units took part under the fitting theme, "Somos Uno,"—We are One. The caucus continued to meet annually as the executive committee of the Fellowship.

The second and third assemblies were held in 1984 and 1986 in San Benito, Texas, and Rochester, New York.

The constitution of the new group emphasized the purposes of (1) unifying Hispanic Disciples, (2) involving Hispanics in denominational decision-making, (3) increasing communication among Hispanics in general, and (4) communicating with Hispanic churches in other parts of the world. Luis E. Ferrer, a Gary, Indiana pastor, who later was to become the director of Hispanic and Bilingual services for the Division of Homeland Ministries, became the first president of the fellowship on June 26, 1981.

During the 1980s the denomination's Church Advance Now program envisioned establishment of ten Hispanic congregations. Anibal Burgos initiated the first new congregation in Queens, New York, with Daisy Machado and Ismael Sanchez the pastor/developers for a new group in Houston, Texas. Samuel Sandoval accepted the challenge in Austin, Texas. Other CAN congregations were planned in Philadelphia, Los Angeles and Lubbock, Texas.

F. Feliberto Pereira redeveloped the San Benito, Texas, church in the far southern Rio Grande valley, then joined the Southwest regional staff as director of Hispanic projects in the Bluebonnet area. Pereira continued a radio ministry to Latin America that reached thousands of persons throughout the area.

Ferdinand Garcia, a layman and cabinet maker from New York, bracketed a lifetime of service to the Disciples of Christ by being elected president in 1987 of the Northeastern junta—nearly 30 years after he had been the junta's first president.

American Asian Disciples

The church had been involved in the concerns of American Asians for some time but the organization of American-Asian Disciples is of recent vintage. The Disciples were among the first church groups in 1942 to protest the injustice done to West Coast Japanese-Americans relocated against their will inland in camps during the war. The call at that time for reparations for those relocated was similar to the 1980s effort by Japanese-Americans to seek redress through Congress.

One of the relocated Japanese-Americans, who lost his electrical contracting business as a result, James Sugioka, came to Indianapolis after the internment to work for the Disciples overseas ministries. He became the purchaser for overseas supplies, ranging from nuts and bolts to airplanes.

More modest in numbers than the other two principal ethnic groups among Disciples, the American Asians met for an Asia Dialogue, July 27-28, 1978, in Indianapolis under the sponsorship of the Division of Homeland Ministries. Harold Johnson of the division staff took a special interest in American Asians and devoted major attention to encouraging and assisting them.

Sixteen persons participated in that 1978 meeting, eleven of them Asians, five general staff. A larger group met the following year in Spencer, Indiana. Noting a desire to "advocate American Asian concerns for the sake of a more effective ministry of the whole church," the group organized a First Convocation of American Asian Disciples for October 6-8, 1980, in Indianapolis. Immigration was the focus.

Twenty American Asians representing Chinese, Filipino, Indonesian, Japanese, Korean and Malaysian heritages took part. David Kagiwada, a pastor in Indianapolis and also a World War II internee, was chosen as the first convener of the group. When American Asian Disciples met in Los Angeles for their fourth convocation in mid-1986, they chose Wallace Ryan Kuroiwa, Youngstown, Ohio, pastor, as their convener.

Kagiwada, the prime mover in American Asian Disciples,

died unexpectedly and a scholarship fund was set up in his memory for the training of American Asian ministers. Soongook Choi, a Chicago area pastor, served on the board of directors of the Division of Homeland Ministries and was the leader of the American Asians in promoting theological education and new congregation establishment.

Asians held three key positions in Disciples staff in the 1980s. The much-loved and widely-known Itoko Maeda was director of interpretation for the Division of Overseas Ministries. Laura Luz Bacerra worked for the church women's department and then became executive secretary for southeast Asia. JoAnne Kagiwada, trained in law, came to the Division of Homeland Ministries staff in 1978 as director of international affairs, serving in 1984 as a member of the church's Panel on Christian Ethics in a Nuclear Age.

Increasing street violence in the United States against Asians, presumed to be influenced by Japanese commercial competition and the loss of jobs plus a residue of anger over the Vietnam war, was a major concern of the group in the 1980s. With the prompting of active American Asians, the General Assembly of the church in Des Moines in 1985 called attention to the issue with a resolution. Citing flagrant examples of the violence and killing, the General Assembly urged Disciples to join in local, regional and national efforts to deal with the violence built on "decades of misperceptions, stereotypes, and notions of cultural and political superiority."

* * *

"Stories of . . . exemplary individuals are an important part of the tradition that is so central to a community of memory."

The concept was simple. If blacks and whites ever were going to love each other, they were going to have to relate—one-to-one, sharing joys and problems and frustrations and fears and successes and the everyday goings-on of life. No patronizing. No holding back. And who best could sympathize with each other's daily grind? Mothers. Black mothers. White mothers. People who take care of children, who try to maintain a home while working.

NORMAN ELLINGTON was one of those people with quiet charisma. You wouldn't have known he had a college degree, but he did. You wouldn't have known he had read theologians and sociologists, but he had. He had a shyness about him, but he was full of stories, very personal stories—about people in need and people helping. Over six feet tall, bald, with a slight mustache and a high pitched voice, generally in a sport shirt, open at the neck, he never talked about himself. He didn't enjoy meetings. He knew they were necessary but occasionally in a tense moment he would stalk out—and have a cigarette. He wasn't particularly interested in the structures of church but occasionally he would acknowledge they were necessary to do effective ministry.

He was God's one-on-one person. He knew somebody everywhere, at home in St. Louis or practically anywhere else he visited. To ride with him in his car and have hopes of arriving somewhere at a given time was frustrating. He would stop, leave the car, and visit with someone on a street corner, telling that person he knew of a job they might be interested in. He would spot vacant houses and try to find out how someone might apply for them. Occasionally he would make detours to a housing project or welfare office. He was constantly popping into phone booths to call someone. When he was out of town, as soon as he would get to his hotel room, he would be on the telephone. Though black, he had many contacts among whites.

He was a staff member of the Missouri state employment security division—until he became staff of the Change Through Involvement program of the Disciples of Christ. Change Through Involvement had its origins in the Division of Homeland Ministries in 1968. Initial funding came through the Irwin-Sweeney-Miller Foundation and the purpose was to relate blacks and whites in unthreatening ways in the hope that deeper involvements would follow naturally.

Ellington and four others in different cities were recruited as staff in 1969 after Ellington and Missouri pastor Thomas O. Russell drafted a response to the urban crisis for state Disciples. Russell became coordinator of the program in Indianapolis. Ellington became the St. Louis operative, tied to the Disciples Council of Greater St. Louis.

Ellington became identified with the most successful part of the program called "Mother-to-Mother." In trying to relate family to family—black and white—it became evident soon that fathers were the most difficult to pin down to participation. But lots of mothers were ready and willing. Rather than make them wait, he began working with the mothers alone. He tried to relate three white suburban mothers with one black welfare mother. There was the risk of overwhelming the black but with three whites there might be a better chance of one white mother and the black mother identifying with each other well. There were to be no lectures, no charity.

The problems black mothers encountered included, of course, child care. One aspect of that was clothes for their children for school. One group of mothers gathered remnants and made clothes for the black children to wear to school. A teacher promptly called the welfare office and the welfare office cut off the mother's checks, thinking she must have been a welfare cheat because the children were so well-dressed. Dealing with issues like that were shocking educations for suburban whites.

Housing was a second concern. White mothers would call about apartments for rent. Then they would go with the welfare mother to secure the apartment—only to find that suddenly once the managers had seen the prospective occupant the apartments already were rented. The welfare mothers were lonesome: they didn't have clubs and committees and entertainment to which their white counterparts were accustomed. And medical needs: welfare mothers didn't know what they were entitled to, didn't know how to ask for services, didn't know how to fill out forms.

Deloris Holt and her husband D. Allison, met Norman Ellington on a visit to Bethany Christian Church. That week Ellington called her. He asked her to coordinate the program. He took her to visit slums, welfare homes, to eat soul food. He explained that he wanted advocacy to come out of learning experiences. He was always conscious that Deloris was white. He would take her into a black situation but not go inside with her, permitting her to develop her own relationships, but he would be standing close by, smoking a cigarette.

The Mother-to-Mother program expanded to 36 cities. More than 1,300 women were involved. Ellington was called to give his own low-key motivational speeches in new locations. He told stories of how individuals had made a difference. He had lots of stories: a black businessman couldn't get a loan. But when a white businessman went with him, the picture changed. No moralizing, just practical illustrations of love across racial lines. "If you're a Christian you're going to love somebody different from you," Ellington explained. "It's easy to love your friends."

Ellington was an admirer of Martin Luther King Jr. Presumably that meant he believed in non-violence. He certainly was non-violent himself. But you could never get him into a discussion about philosophical or theological positions. He was non-doctrinaire. He believed in living the Christian gospel, not discussing it. "If you're free in Christ, you're free to love—free to love across racial and economic lines." He said it everywhere to mother-to-mother groups he was organizing. It was about as doctrinaire as Ellington ever got.

Ellington told Tom Russell the story: He once picked up a white man, drunk in the gutter. He took him home and got him cleaned up. When the white expressed appreciation, Ellington said, "You're a doctor, aren't you?" "Yes, how did you know?" "I remember you. Years ago I came to your door and you refused me service. I forgive you."

In the spring of 1974 Norman Ellington died. He had Hodgkins disease. He never complained, but he had wasted away for about a year. He still traveled on Mother-to-Mother projects before he died. But he was thin and he would lie down while in conversation and he would go to bed early to satisfy a spent body—and a well-spent spirit.

7

The Ministry:
Architects of Identity

1971—*Charles Manson convicted* (Jan. 26) . . . *Supreme Court okays busing* (April 20) . . . UCMS reorganizes into Homeland Ministries and Overseas Ministries divisions . . . *Pentagon Papers published* (June 13) . . . Louisville Assembly adopts chalice as symbol (October 15-20) . . . *26th amendment lowers voting age to 18* (Oct. 25) . . . Structure committee proposes larger and fewer regions . . . Disciples, UCC overseas boards meet together 1st time to discuss joint administration.

1972—*Nixon visits China* (Feb. 21) . . . *North Vietnam launches biggest attacks in four years* (March 30) . . . *George Wallace wounded* (May 15) . . . *Nixon signs arms pact in Moscow* (May 22) . . . General Board urges end to Cuba embargo (June 10-13) . . . *Watergate break-in* (June 17) . . . *Supreme Court says no to death penalty* (June 29) . . . *Last U.S. combat troops leave Vietnam* (Aug. 11) . . . *Israeli athletes killed at Munich Olympics* (Sept. 5) . . . Bingham leads Asia fraternal visit (October).

Kenneth Teegarden, General Minister and President 1973-85, always said that the best way to describe the chief executive office of the Disciples of Christ was "A. Dale Fiers." People automatically assumed that Fiers would be the first General Minister and President of the restructured church, just as perhaps the United States forefathers assumed no one but George Washington could have been first. Fiers was the commander in chief. He had headed the United Christian Missionary Society and the International Convention of Christian Churches.

In the early restructure talks the chief executive was called simply the "president." As discussion revolved around whether the position would be administrative or pastoral, the answer was both. The restructure commission wanted someone to be the chief of staff of the church at the general level. But this was a spiritual leader too—a pastor to the whole church. Fiers certainly fit that description. And the double title gradually came into being.

It was a unique title. There were a few other double titles in the chief executive's spot in American Christendom, a couple of them embracing administrative and pastoral responsibilities. But no other "general minister and president." The general minister part of it preceded the president to underscore where Disciples placed their emphasis. They wanted a pastor to the church.

The *Design for the Christian Church (Disciples of Christ)* is not specific about the duties of the General Minister and President. Mostly it describes how she/he is elected and how long the GMP serves. The General Minister and President is "concerned for the pastoral care and nurture" of the church and presides over the general staff. The only other prescribed duty is to "represent the (Disciples) in interchurch relations and in ecumenical circles." The General Minister serves six-year terms until age 65. The Administrative Committee of the General Board, when it spelled out procedures for selecting a General Minister and President in 1972 and 1984, gave a little more of a clue as to what the expected function was: to preach, to lead, to give vision, to speak to the church and the world, to bring theological convictions to bear on issues, to articulate the faith with clarity and power, to set objectives and develop strategy, to inspire confidence.

Dr. Fiers was retiring in 1973 and it came time to select a successor. The process was a long one. The 44-member Administrative Committee, the 250-member General Board and the multi-thousand voting representatives at General Assembly each had to approve the person by a two-thirds vote. Since the General Board met three months prior to the General Assembly and the Administrative Committee three to five months prior to that, the total process including receiving recommendations from the constituency, screening the candidates down to an interviewable number, conducting interviews and recommending three to five persons to the Administrative Committee consumed about a year and a half.

When the time came to find a successor to Fiers, two prime prospects emerged. One was Kenneth Teegarden, then regional minister of Texas, the church's largest. The other was Thomas J. Liggett, deputy to Dr. Fiers following service as the president of UCMS. True to form, neither of the two indicated—at least publicly—any interest in the position. In fact, while the Administrative Committee was deliberating behind closed doors before settling on the specific nomination, the Teegardens and Liggetts were traveling together to Asia.

Teegarden had served earlier as an aide to Dr. Fiers, administering the restructure process. He had been a prime drafter of the document. His reputation was as a skillful negotiator with a legal mind (he had once intended to become a lawyer), attention to details, superb organizer, warm pastor and quiet administrator.

Liggett, former missionary to Argentina and president of a Puerto Rican seminary, had served as the Latin America secretary before becoming president of the UCMS. He was a superb administrator, an internationally-recognized theologian, liberal activist and brilliant commentator on the social scene. The Administrative Committee deliberated behind closed doors for eight hours trying to choose between the two. Teegarden emerged as the choice. He became General Minister and President in October 1973.

While Kenneth Teegarden may have thought that the position of General Minister and President described Dale Fiers, it was Teegarden himself who in the next 12 years incarnated the position for Disciples. He carefully built a strong collegial relationship among the general and regional executives and one of trust. He never pretended an authority he didn't have and he never took himself too seriously though he was flawless diplomatically in ceremonial functions and relationships. He planned meetings down to the last detail and his dockets and agendas were polished. He was a committed ecumenist and in 1975 he encouraged the resumption of union conversations with the United Church of Christ. He spoke and wrote forcefully on issues of the day—always carefully within established policy of the General Assembly—and he projected "peace with justice" into the Disciples' consciences as the priority of the 1980s. There was always a relaxed dignity about him. Basically shy, Teegarden preferred one-to-one encounters as opposed to group meetings, although he moderated the latter well.

Order of Ministry

The General Minister and President is the chief minister in a denomination with a history of distrust of professional clergy. Alexander Campbell felt that ministers ought to have regular jobs and preach and minister out of conviction only. At times he railed about the "hireling" clergy. Easy for him to say: he married well and his own needs were taken care of so that he did not have to make a living and could tend to spiritual things alone. W. T. Moore in 1909 described the Disciples as first and foremost "a protest against the reign of priestcraft and religious despotism."

Nevertheless, over the years the Disciples had come to a rather high appreciation of a trained ministry. Many Disciples were hopeful that restructure would help set some standards for being a part of the church's ministry. No one denied that congregations had the right to call their own ministers. But did the congregation's right to call also give it the right to ordain persons into the ministry of the whole church?

That was a tougher question. Shouldn't there be some broader authority with greater access to resources to evaluate the capabilities and qualifications of ministers? Shouldn't there be some body able to recommend ministers to congregations and some means to identify and oust from the denominational accepted list those not fit?

The latter question always raised nervousness about freedom of the pulpit and the danger of abuse of the power to identify and oust. So an Order of the Ministry was one of the matters left incomplete in the adoption of restructure. The matter simply was too difficult politically to tackle in the context of securing approval for a major restructure of the denomination.

The *Design* did have a section on ministry. It emphasized the ministry of the whole people. It recognized an "Order of Ministry," which was new to Disciples, that included ordained and licensed ministers, offices which were not new. It gave the regions the role of certifying the standing of ministers serving within their regions. It gave to the General Assembly the responsibility of setting policies and criteria for the order—criteria relating to commitment, character, education, standing, ethics, placement and support, but the *Design* itself did not include any of those policies. It left to the region the administration of the policies and the determination who fits the criteria.

Soon after restructure, the General Board appointed a Task Force on the Ministry. For two years the Task Force labored. At the 1971 General Assembly in Louisville there was a document on the Order of the Ministry. Noting that all Christians share in ministry the Policies and Criteria document justified the Order of the Ministry as having led "in transmitting the Christian tradition from one generation to another," coming as close as Disciples would dare to espousing an apostolic succession. Among the qualifications required of those in the Order of the Ministry are "mental and physical capacities, emotional stability and maturity, and standards of morality."

Qualifications for the Order

The document specified that admission to the Order of the Ministry required theological and professional study, ethical principles and "growth in personal character, Christian insight, spiritual formation, and disciplined commitment to ministry."

Though the early days of the Disciples of Christ saw an aversion to theological training for ministers, the Policies and Procedures specified that ordained ministers "ordinarily" should have an undergraduate degree and a seminary program of study. Some ministers even in the present day do not have seminary educations, 20 percent of the ministers serving congregations in 1985 essentially being preachers whose livings are earned in work outside the church.

The *Design* says the regions "help" the congregations in ordination. The policies document specifically assigns to regions the authorizing of ordination and the supervising of the act of ordaining. The document also reviews reasons for the termination of standing of ministers, the reasons including failure to perform faithfully the duties authorized by ordination or licensing, failure to grow educationally and spiritually, and not maintaining relationships with the Christian Church (Disciples of Christ) or active membership in one of its congregations "where feasible." Listing in the *Year Book and Directory* of the church officially conveys standing under the policies and criteria. In practice, the official listing has been in the department of the ministry of the Division of Homeland Ministries.

Additions have been made to the policies on the Order of the Ministry over the years since its 1971 adoption by the Louisville General Assembly. In 1977 the Assembly revised it to include criteria and procedures for candidacy. Ministerial candidates under the policy must have the support of a congregation, apply to the region and be assessed by the region as to "spiritual, emotional, moral intellectual and educational capacities."

In 1981, ministerial standing policies were revised. The revisions made certain (l) that all ministers have an accountability, whether serving in congregations or not, (2) that ministers in standing must be employed by or seeking employment from the church, and (3) that they must continue to meet the qualifications of their original admittance to the ministry.

In 1985 at the Des Moines General Assembly, the Disciples added a new section to their Policies and Criteria for the Order of the Ministry. That was a section on "ministerial relocation." In the section, the Disciples reaffirm the right of the church at all levels to call ministers to particular tasks and the full freedom of ministers to accept or reject calls to service. Among the principles stated in the section is one that insists that congregations "strive" to be open to considering all minister candidates, regardless of race, ethnic origin, sex, age or physical disability. Further, "congregations may talk with a number of ministers concurrently, but will negotiate with only one minister at a time."

Ministerial Standing Most Difficult

Joyce Coalson, executive secretary of the department of ministry, observed in 1987 that ministerial standing has been the most difficult Order of the Ministry issue for Disciples to deal with. In a paper prepared for a conference on the Disciples' future she said: "The fears that regions would be arbitrary in the granting and removing of ministerial standing have proven to be ungrounded. Careful and thorough procedures have been set up with the built-in safeguard of right of appeal to the General Board Task Force on Ministerial Standing."

Coalson indicated further she believed that the regional commissions on the ministry are doing their jobs responsibly and well. Theirs was a heavy load of interviewing and decision-making with regard to licensing, ordination and standing. The number of Disciples ministers seeking relocation was at an all-time high when she spoke—nearly 14 percent of the ministers serving congregations.

The 1986 *Year Book* included the names of 6,886 ministers with standing. That figure compared with 7,428 in the unofficial list just prior to restructure. The pre-restructure list represented an "open and inviting" list. While the number of ministers with standing in 1986 was 7 percent less than the pre-restructure informal listing, the number of congregations listed in the book just prior to restructure and in 1986 was down 28 percent—the full number of withdrawals over restructure not having been completed at that time. Of those 6,886 ministers in the church in 1986, 23 percent were retired. Forty six percent were serving fulltime on the staffs of congregations, 10 percent were in other employment but preaching. The remaining 21 percent were chaplains, missionaries, higher education ministers, ministerial specialists, ecumenical ministers or staffs of regions or the general church.

As might be expected, the percentage of Disciples ministers in retirement rose sharply over the 18-year period. In 1967 only 16 percent of the list represented retirees. The number of ministers earning their living from secular employment declined two percent.

Women in the mid-1980s represented some 12 percent of the total ministry of the church (up from 4 percent in 1973). But in the seminaries they had grown to 40 percent of the student bodies (9 percent in 1973). It left Disciples with major decisions to make about how to better convince congregations of the viability of calling women pastors.

Coalson, in her paper on the future of the ministry for Disciples, offered a hint that a change of gender might involve renewal of the church as well. "At the heart of this issue for women is not simply finding places to serve. It is finding places to serve that will call forth their gifts and celebrate them rather than demand that they mold themselves into the forms and styles of their male predecessors and peers."

When in 1986 the Division of Homeland Ministries took a major survey of more than 13,000 Disciples, a part of it had to do with the relationship between congregations and their ministers. Ann Updegraff-Spleth, vice president of DHM, reported that 84 percent of the respondents to a written survey felt that their minister was "happy and satisfied" in his/her job (3 percent reported a "her"). But nearly a third said there had been serious conflict between the minister and the congregation.

The process of naming a new General Minister and President in 1985 to succeed Kenneth Teegarden drew criticism from some members of the Administrative Committee. As a result a task force chaired by John R. Bean, pastor in Columbus, Indiana, meticulously worked out changes, including shortening the process to a year and assuring that general staff are not in a position to influence the outcome. But, in terms of the ministry of the Christian Church (Disciples of Christ), the significant change was to bar lay persons from serving in the office of General Minister and President. The argument was that the church does not recommend persons without training in ministry as local pastors. It should not call a lay person to be the church's chief minister, the pastor to the whole church.

Several years into Teegarden's service as General Minister and President, noted theologian Martin Marty was asking in *Christian Century* magazine what had happened to all the great church leaders of the 1950s and 1960s. He speculated that few of his readers could even recognize the names of mainline Protestantism's current presidents and he listed six names. Teegarden's name was among them. Teegarden told his wife Wanda that Marty had included him in the list of unknown denominational chief executives. After listening patiently, Wanda Teegarden inquired: "Who is Martin Marty?"

Three Offices of Ministry

In 1985 the Disciples' Commission on Theology (related to the Council on Christian Unity) proposed that Disciples consider three offices of ministry, rather than the present designations of ordained and licensed in its order of ministry. The three would be the ministry of service, or deacon, the ministry of proclamation of word and sacrament, or pastor, and the ministry of oversight, or bishop. The three-fold ministry concept had been pondered by theologians and others of various Christian groups for at least 20 years in ecumenical circles.

The commission explained that the three offices not only had historic precedent in Christendom and a solid theological foundation, but would be a way for ecumenically-oriented churches to reconcile their ministries and embrace the church's functions of service, proclamation, mission and unity. Said the commission: "In each of the offices of the three-fold ordained ministry being proposed, one aspect of the church's life and witness comes into particular focus: In the ministry of the deacon, the active witness and mission of the church as servant is assisted and advanced. In the ministry of the presbyter, the proclamation, preaching, teaching, and sacramental dimensions (presiding at the Table and administering baptism) of the church are lifted up. In the ministry of the bishop, the oversight of the life of the community comes into focus."

Since Disciples over the years have had difficulty with the idea of bishops, the 20-member theology commission elaborated on the New Testament *episkopos*. The Apostle Paul used the term borrowed from the Greco-Roman where it represented economic oversight. Alexander Campbell used the term as an equal to "elders" of the congregation responsible for shepherding, teaching, leading and ministering. Disciples, the commission said, constantly exercise the ministry of oversight, at all levels, and by a wide variety of people, including local "shepherding" programs.

"Any understanding and practice of *episcope* among Disciples must be developed in terms of its ministerial and pastoral functions," the commission reported to the General Assembly, "and not in relation to magisterial or hierarchical exercise of authority. In the best of situations regional ministers function collegially and exercise authority as that of a 'shepherd' or 'pastor to pastors.'"

A Beautiful Moment for Bingham

It was most appropriate that during this period of developing an order of ministry the Moderator should be a much loved local pastor. Walter D. Bingham of Louisville, Kentucky, for many people was the quintessential pastor: gentle, thoughtful, spiritual, wise, sensitive, prayerful, socially aware. He had a penetrating and non-judgmental way of interpreting black perceptions to whites. In May 1973, five months before the General Assembly over which he would preside as Moderator, Bingham checked into the Peabody Hotel in Memphis—a prime suite befitting the Moderator—for the opening of the meeting of the Consultation on Church Union.

The historic old Peabody Hotel was noted for its "duck walk." There was a fountain in the lobby in which ducks frolicked during the daytime hours. The ducks arrived every morning at eight by hotel elevator and departed each afternoon at four. Their coming and going was an event. With a bit of taped musical fanfare, the elevator doors would open precisely at eight, the bellman would have rolled out a red carpet from the elevator to the fountain, and the ducks would waddle out single file to the fountain never straying from the carpet.

At the end of the day, they would sense that it was time to go home to their pen on the roof and they would stand on the edge of the fountain waiting their carpet and the music and their private elevator home. It was a spectacle that drew residents of the hotel and persons off the street daily to the Peabody lobby.

But this day in 1973 at the Peabody was a special moment in the life of Walter Bingham. Thirty-five years earlier Bingham was a busboy, cleaning up tables in that hotel, and he wouldn't have been allowed to stay in the Peabody, much less in the honored suite. He waited for the bellman to open his door and deposit his bag in the corner of the suite with a big smile on his face. It was a special kind of "first" for Walter Bingham.

Walter Bingham was the first black Moderator for the Disciples. He was elected in 1971 at the Louisville General Assembly without opposition, although there was a nervous moment handled skillfully by John R. Compton, the staff director of Reconciliation. Prior to Bingham's nomination and before the bulk of the Assembly knew that he was black, there was a floor discussion about the need for a woman Moderator. Some feminist speeches followed, including the suggestion that a woman nominated for Vice-Moderator ought to be shifted to the top position.

The matter seemed to be settling down toward Bingham's nomination when an elderly black woman preacher headed down the center aisle presumably to join the issue on behalf of a woman. Compton, seeing her approaching the microphone, rose from his aisle seat, met her at mid-aisle, linked his arm in hers and as the two of them reached the cross-aisle just before the microphone, gently did a left-flank movement with her away from the microphone and out of the auditorium for a friendly chat! The Assembly roared with amusement.

Bingham was noted at denominational meetings for his sensitive and thoughtful expositions of scripture. He enjoyed keeping members of the Administrative Committee and General Board alert when he was presiding by altering the form of the yea-nay vote. Sometimes he would call for a "oui" or "non," or a "si" or "no," or a "da" or "nyet," and occasionally a colloquial like a "right on" or "no suh!"

One of his most endearing bits of humor came at the 1973 General Board meeting in St. Louis when he announced he would like certain board members to introduce particular resolutions. For instance, he said, all financial matters should be handled by

Jackie Buck, Albert Pennybacker, Keith Nichols and Tom Money. Environmental issues should be dealt with by Ellison Lakes, Susan Bush, Richard Flowers, A. C. Stone and Darrell Wood. Violence questions were to go to Lawrence Bash and Mrs. W. W. Thrasher. Finally, any Vietnam matters he wanted debated by Dennis Savage and Jimmy Gentle!

* * *

"Stories of . . . exemplary individuals are an important part of the tradition that is so central to a community of memory."

"Most people do evangelism in a self-centered way; They try to get people into the church. Evangelism is not about the church growing. It is loving people. If it grows, that's secondary."

That philosophy sounds like a cop-out you might hear from someone in a non-growing church. Hardly. When C. WILLIAM NICHOLS, who expressed it, arrived in Decatur, Illinois, from Kansas January 1, 1973, to be the pastor of Central Christian Church, there were 1,983 participating members. By 1987 there were 2,705, despite Central's being a downtown congregation and the "Soy Capital" having a population that remained constant.

The Decatur newspaper called Central "the friendliest church in town." Says Nichols: "We care about every person who walks in the door." An out-of-state occasional visitor recalled with appreciation, "He remembered my name." A Muslim woman from Iran came down the aisle in tears to join the church, saying that it was what she had been looking for all her life. A parishioner said: "He's a good friend to people." Another: "The congregation cares so deeply about him that anything he mentions is done." Still another: "Everything he does is with kindness and understanding. No blame."

The church was instrumental in reconciling a non-member of the congregation (through its radio program and followup) with her parents after a long enmity. Nichols can call most of the 90 nursery school children by name as they pass his office. Portly and with striking blond hair and mustache, the pastor has a communicable smile, a sly wit, and a spirit that seems incapable of being ruffled.

The congregation's weekly half-hour radio program called

"Good News from Central" returned to a listener a check that he wrote. Good news comes through the media with no strings attached and no guilt feelings allowed! Nichols delivers a traditional message on the 50,000 watt WSOY but one that is tailored to a radio audience and there is no broadcast of worship services—he believes the worship service has meaning only in context of the church setting.

Someone referred to Central's facility as the busiest building in town. Nichols' philosophy is "fit the church program to the community need." As a result, Decatur Central has a major economic justice program called DOVE, also a roughly $50,000 a year rescue fund to assist community agencies suffering from government cutbacks, a $15-20,000 a year emergency fund to pay utility bills, groceries and clothing for needy persons. The church makes no judgment about who is needy. "Anybody who is hungry deserves to be fed," explains Nichols. "There are no undeserving poor." There are health and well-being classes, effective parenting programs, evolution and creationism discussions, divorce and grief clinics, and French, Spanish, Italian, Swedish, German and Russian classes. Why the particular languages? "Someone expressed a need."

When an elementary school was damaged in a tragic railyard explosion, Central offered the church as a meeting place. The school brought 315 students to the church daily. Never mind that there was a 90-child nursery already in the building, plus the classes and nine church choirs.

Nichols doesn't like to see Christians permit church property to deteriorate; they wouldn't do so with their businesses or homes. Decatur Central in 1987 was making a $1.8 million addition to its 1955 plant, especially with children's program in mind. Nichols also believes sloppy worship services depress people who have been exposed to masterful media entertainment. The church should be exciting, and willing to "go against the grain."

Nichols loves to preach, saying people are hungry to hear good sermons. The sermons are printed and made available in the vestibule to anyone who wants a copy, donation or not. One of the church members marvels that while the sermons are in manuscript form, Nichols never uses the manuscript or even notes. He spends hours rehearsing as well as writing his sermons.

When Central recruits personnel to do congregation tasks, it recruits with a personal visit and with full particulars as to the scope and the joys of the task. Never are people told the task won't take much time. They are told it could be one of the great satisfactions of their lives.

Nichols was born October 2, 1927, in Baxter Springs, a southeastern Kansas town of 4,000 that is almost a suburb of Joplin, Missouri. He studied two years at Kansas State College and then earned a B.A. at Culver-Stockton in Canton, Missouri. He earned a divinity degree at Phillips University, which also gave him an honorary doctorate in 1975. He served pastorates in Poteau, Oklahoma, and Augusta, Kansas, before a seven-year ministry in Kansas City, Kansas. Nichols and wife Claudine have two children, a son who is an attorney in Tulsa and a daughter who is in Decatur, serving as an elder and a Sunday School teacher in the church.

Though Nichols has a good staff, he spreads himself widely. A member of a church family was experiencing open heart surgery in Springfield, Illinois. It was sudden and traumatic. The night before the surgery in Springfield, Nichols was at the hospital, sensitive and reassuring. Another heart case: the pastor had just returned from an out-of-town trip. He was tired but immediately upon learning of the hospitalization he was on the scene. "I know the surgeon," he said. "You've got the best." The patient had one chance in three. Nichols asked to be informed how things went. At 2:00 a.m. he received a call: The surgery was a success. "I have just been lying here, awake, waiting for your call," he said.

Often the church that is growing does so by turning inward on itself. It lacks a sense of outreach. Nichols does not tolerate that kind of thinking. He goes back to his statement on self-centered evangelism. "Outreach," he says, "is evangelism on a global scale." In 1985 the Decatur Central church gave more than $130,000 to denominational programs, over and above that given to their local outreach ministries. Of that, nearly $100,000 went undesignated to Basic Mission Finance for general distribution, the second highest total among the 4,000-plus Disciples of Christ congregations. At the same time the congregation reported 24 baptisms and 79 total additions. The congregation consistently is among the top growing Disciples communities.

Pastor Nichols looks with optimism on the future of the Disciples of Christ: "The best days of the church are ahead!"

8

The Laity: Foundation for Identity

1973—LBJ funeral at National City Christian Church (Jan. 22) . . . *Supreme Court permits abortion* (Jan. 22) . . . *Military draft ended* (Jan 27) . . . *Indians seize Wounded Knee* (Feb. 27) . . . COCU shifts union effort from plan to process (April 2-6) . . . *Haldeman, Erlichman resign* (April 30) . . . *Brezhnev visits U.S.* (June 16-25) . . . *Egypt/Syria attack Israel* (Oct. 6) . . . *Vice-President Agnew resigns* (Oct. 10) . . . *Arabs block oil to U.S.* (Oct. 19) . . . Teegarden succeeds Fiers at Cincinnati Assembly (Oct. 26-31) . . . *Egypt/ Israel accord* (Nov. 11).

1974—World Call/Christian merge as *The Disciple* (January) . . . *Patty Hearst kidnapped* (Feb. 5) . . . Quadrennial draws 4,156 women (June 24-28) . . . Unified Promotion becomes Church Finance Council (July 1) . . . Wilsons arrested in Philippines (July 26) . . . *Nixon resigns* (Aug. 9) . . . Texas, New Mexico combine into Southwest region . . . *CIA accused of massive domestic operations* (Dec. 21).

1975—Mitchell, Haldeman, others guilty (Jan. 1) . . . Missouri region challenges Finance Commission (April) . . . *U.S. civilians evacuated from Vietnam* (Apr. 29) . . . Disciples Higher Education task force appointed (May) . . . *Mayaguez rescue kills 38 marines* (May 15) . . . *U.S./Soviet satellites link in space* (July 15) . . . San Antonio Assembly OKs mutual recognition of members (Aug. 15-20) . . . *Ford escapes Sacramento assassin* (Sept. 5) . . . *Ford escapes 2nd assassin* (Sept. 22) . . . *Franco dies* (December).

When 4,156 women of the Christian Church (Disciples of Christ) gathered for their fifth quadrennial assembly on the campus of Purdue University in 1974, few Disciples would have disputed that here perhaps was the core strength of the church, all in one place at one time. For the most part, these were the best informed, most committed of the church's constituency. Their fellowship group offerings alone represented one fifth of the total world outreach dollars of the Disciples. They were the spiritual descendants of Disciples women who initiated successful overseas mission work when the men had failed, founded the "Bible Chairs" for teaching religion at public universities which, in turn, resulted in the first campus ministry, built what has been described as the first graduate school of missions in the United States and brought more than half of the institutional resources into the merger of six entities that became the United Christian Missionary Society.

The International Christian Women's Fellowship in 1974 was celebrating 100 years of organized women's work in the church. Also in 1974, the Disciples of Christ were functioning under their first woman Moderator in the United States and Canada, and the lay men of the church were planning an unprecedented international gathering. It was a time for the laity to celebrate their singular contributions to the Disciples of Christ.

The Disciples from the church's beginnings on the frontier prided themselves on being a lay-oriented movement. Part of it was the American rugged individualism rebelling against the clericalism of Europe. Part was the nature of a new movement—without religious training institutions from which to recruit leaders. Part also was the desire to restore the unity of the church by harkening back to New Testament simplicity, a simplicity that some nineteenth and twentieth century Christians idealized as having no need for religious hierarchy.

There were no distinctions in early Disciples churches. Congregations had a plurality of "elders." One of those elders was the teaching elder, or the minister. While the elders may have been ordained by congregations through the laying on of hands, they were not seminary trained. Neither were most of the pastors. Disciples prided themselves on putting the Lord's Supper at the center of worship where it could be celebrated whether an ordained minister was present or not. Some took pride in the view that ANY lay persons could be the celebrants, even youths, without special authorization. The supper was the feast of the Lord and nothing stood in the way of the people at large sharing in this remembrance, thanksgiving and rededication.

Laity in Early Disciples Life

Lay persons had been at the forefront throughout Disciples life and work. Virginia physician James T. Barclay was the church's first missionary in 1852, a mission to Jerusalem that failed. Iowa's Caroline Neville Pearre initiated the first successful missionary organization in 1874, opening the Disciples longest continuing

115

missionary relationship two years later in Jamaica. Ohio physician Robert Richardson settled down at Bethany to do the editing for the last 30 years of Alexander Campbell's life so that Campbell could spend his time traveling and promoting the cause. Interestingly, what is described by historians William Tucker and Lester McAllister as the most widely used "systematic theology" of the Disciples of Christ is a book written in 1868 by Robert Milligan, a Disciples math teacher with no formal training in theology.

Kansas City lumberman R. A. Long, for whom the town of Longview, Washington, is named, initiated the first Disciples laymen's national organization in 1908. What's more he bought a publishing house in St. Louis and gave the Christian Board of Publication its start. Anna R. Atwater negotiated the merger of the missionary societies in 1920 from her position as president of the Christian Woman's Board of Missions, becoming the vice-president of the new society. J. Irwin Miller in 1960 became the first lay person of any denomination to become president of the National Council of Churches.

Caroline Neville Pearre and her friends put together the Christian Woman's Board of Missions in 1874 after the American Christian Missionary Society, organized at the first convention in 1849, met with less than success in Jerusalem and Liberia. The Woman's Board began work in Jamaica in 1876, in India in 1881, Mexico in 1885, Puerto Rico in 1900, Argentina in 1905, and Paraguay in 1918—all work resulting in churches that continue to this day.

In cooperation with the Foreign Christian Missionary Society (the third of the major Disciples missionary societies to organize), the women began work in Africa in 1907 and China in 1915. In the homeland, they started work among southern blacks in 1881, evangelization in Montana in 1883, mission to Chinese on the West Coast in 1884, mountain schools in Kentucky (1886)-West Virginia (1900)-Tennessee (1909), service to Japanese in Los Angeles (1908), and a mission for Mexicans in San Antonio (1913). They began the Bible Chair movement at the University of Michigan in 1893.

On August 29, 1907, they broke ground in Indianapolis for the new graduate school of missions in connection with Butler University, a Disciples institution. The four-story building dedicated August 18, 1910, also housed the CWBM offices. When Butler University moved in 1928 the merged missionary societies, now called the United Christian Missionary Society, occupied the building. The facility still stood in 1987 at 222 South Downey Avenue in East Indianapolis as part of the headquarters complex of the Christian Church (Disciples of Christ).

Women Held Half of UCMS Assets

When the United Christian Missionary Society came into being the women's organization brought into the union 53 percent of the assets, more than the five others combined. The women's *Missionary Tidings* magazine, which had a subscription list of 54,000, was merged with the magazines of the other missionary societies and agencies—their subscriptions were 36,000 total—as *World Call*. *World Call* continued as a journal until restructure when it was merged with *The Christian* to form the current church publication *The Disciple*. In addition to the CWBM in the UCMS merger were the American Christian Missionary Society, the Foreign Christian Missionary Society, the National Benevolent Association, the Board of Church Extension and the Board of Ministerial Relief (now the Pension Fund). The UCMS became for the next 50 years the center of Disciples world activity.

It should be noted in all of this that the women of the United States did not even have the right to vote in elections until August 26, 1920. The UCMS merger arrangement, worked out the year prior to the granting of women's suffrage, included the election of a board that would be 50 percent male and 50 percent female. That assured a strong lay representation since the bulk of the females would not be ordained. The arrangement also was to have one male and one female as the president and vice-president of the Society. That 50-50 division continues to the present day in the divisions of Homeland Ministries and Overseas Ministries that once constituted the two main arms of the UCMS.

The boards of the two have equal male and female representation. (Disciples in General Assembly in 1985 called upon all manifestations of the church to "have equal representation of women and men on their boards.") The Divisions of Homeland and Overseas Ministries have presidents that happen to be male (as the arrangement always seemed to work out following the 1920 agreement) and vice-presidents that are female. Four years after the beginning of the UCMS, Disciples women celebrated their golden anniversary of organization—and coincidentally demonstrated their economic power—by raising an extra million dollars to build 50 new buildings at home and abroad.

Enthusiastic Local Groups

Having enthusiastic local constituency groups is what made the CWBM powerful. Likewise bringing these constituencies into the UCMS provided a strong underpinning for the new united society. Local women's groups became auxiliaries to the new UCMS and were often referred to locally as "the auxiliary," or later the Women's Missionary Society. But there also were Women's Councils and Ladies' Aid Societies in local churches. Sometimes these women's groups competed with each other in the same congregation.

Theoretically, local women were linked together with each other and with the world through the UCMS department of missionary organizations. Headed by Jessie Trout, that department called for a conference January 8-17, 1949, in Turkey Run State Park in Indiana to deal with the frequent confusion of roles in the churches among Ladies' Aids, Women's Councils and women's Missionary Societies. A total of seventy-five women met at Turkey Run and created the Christian Women's Fellowship—a women's organization with functional departments of worship, study and service, an arrangement that continues to the present. July 1, 1950, was the official launch date for the new CWF.

The organizing of two bodies—the world and the international—came next. It should be made clear that the International Christian Women's Fellowship is the organization of women in the United States and Canada. The WORLD Christian Women's Fellowship is that fellowship of women of the Disciples of Christ tradition in more than a dozen countries around the world. The World Christian Women's Fellowship had its origins at the World Convention of Churches of Christ in Melbourne, Australia, in 1952. Jessie Trout, visiting various countries on her way to Australia, found a strong desire for such a fellowship, which became a reality three years later.

The United States and Canada organization, on the other hand, dates to the 1953 International Convention in Portland, Oregon. There just prior to the convention opening two thousand women met and launched the International Christian Women's Fellowship. By 1957 the huge mission offerings collected by women, which previously had been earmarked entirely for the UCMS, became a part of Unified Promotion, with distribution to all agencies of the church on the same basis as other outreach offerings. When the first Quadrennial Assembly was held in 1957, some 3,500 women took part.

Jessie Trout Founds Quadrennial

The Quadrennial idea also germinated with Jessie Trout in the early 1950s. Trout had been a missionary to Japan for 20 years. She came to the United Society staff in 1946. She saw the tremendous value of contact among women and their influence upon the ministry of the church. That first Quadrennial took place at Purdue in 1957 just a year before the Disciples' restructure need was articulated by Willard Wickizer. Quadrennial was an immediate success. It was called Quadrennial because the intent was to hold it every four years even though the gap between the second and third Quadrennials was five. That one was delayed a year so as not to conflict with the World Convention of Churches of Christ in Puerto Rico.

Each Quadrennial since has been marked by growing participation and enthusiasm. The Quadrennial serves notice on the church that the women are well-schooled in the issues of the day and the needs and ministries of the church and that they will be a financial force to be reckoned with. Over the years the women's fellowship groups—more than 3,200 of them—have provided some 20 percent of the church's entire Basic Mission Finance. That support has grown to where it amounts to more than $3 million annually, though the percentage of the total Disciples outreach is now down to 18 percent. The number of women participating in CWF declined as the church membership dropped. But the 1986 figures still showed 143,000 women involved in CWF groups. One reason for the large CWF financial support of the church's mission is the concentration in program studies on outreach in addition to personal enrichment.

Helen F. Spaulding succeeded Jessie Trout in 1961 as the church's CWF executive just as the Restructure Era was beginning. Spaulding became a major contributor on the restructure commission and its task committees. The following year the

Christian Women's Fellowship reached a long sought-after goal of providing $2 million in a single year to the world outreach budget of the church.

The Quadrennial Assemblies always have been much attuned to the social setting of the times in which they are held. In 1961 the women struggled with the importance of individual choices in vocations, stewardship and relation to others. In 1966 they faced the turbulence of the times: war and peace, poverty and affluence, human rights and encouraging women to deeper involvement in church and community. Four years later the focus was on Christian hope and actions leading to change. In the 1970s as women's rights and inclusiveness came to the fore, those issues became the focus of Quadrennial. In 1978, just prior to the International Year of the Child, the women took on the concern for infant malnutrition in the third world.

Efforts at Combining Laity

A 1968 consultation on Women in the Church recommended continuing flexibility in organizational matters, study-with-action goals, closer working of Christian Women's Fellowship and Christian Men's Fellowship in planning program materials, and the cooperative use of leadership at the general level. The talk of a closer relationship with lay men was born not only of considerations of costs of producing resources and the desire to coordinate program for the whole church, but a condition in society when traditional male-female groupings were crumbling in favor of more interchange. There was serious consideration in 1969 of merger of the men's and women's fellowships. But just as the society influenced the initiation of such consideration, society took a turn that brought an end to it.

The years 1970-71 were years in which the women's movement came into strong focus, years in which women affirmed themselves and developed their own goals for realizing potential. It was not a time when merger with male-oriented structures would have furthered the female affirmation. So the separate structures were left intact. An experimental Lay Advisory Council that bridged the female-male constituency structures continued until 1982.

The year prior to the celebration of the 100th anniversary of women's work, 1973, the support arm in the Division of Homeland Ministries in Indianapolis changed its name from the department of Christian Women's Fellowship to the department of Church Women. The change was to dramatize that the general structure was to provide resources to all women of the church, not only those that identified with CWF. In June 1979 the Division of Homeland Ministries approved an Action Research Project which resulted in the founding in 1983 of a Church Women's Coordinating Council to bring the non-CWF women into the women's planning structures.

The 1973 Assembly in Cincinnati elected Jean Woolfolk of Little Rock, Arkansas, as the first woman Moderator but it also dealt with five resolutions initiated by the women of the church: One stressed the office of deacon in the church as being for females as well as males, encouraging congregations in the direction of a single diaconate rather than separate boards of deacons and deaconesses. Another called for study of abortion issues and support of persons who made abortion decisions, whichever way. Two of them dealt with encouragement to women to enter the ministry, urging congregations to consider hiring them—for compensation equivalent to that of male ministers. The General Assembly endorsed an Equal Rights Amendment to the United States Constitution as well, observing: "While admitting that it has not always lived up to its own teachings, the church has long proclaimed that laws and practices which prevent women from exercising their freedom as children of God are morally indefensible."

At the 1974 Quadrennial the women elected their first black president, Carnella Barnes of Los Angeles. That August 14, Helen Spaulding retired and was succeeded January 1, 1975, by Fran Craddock, a member of the church's General Board and the Acting Moderator of the region of Illinois-Wisconsin.

A 1985 General Assembly resolution on the leadership of women in the Disciples of Christ proposed a 50-50 split of male and female board members throughout the church, a recommendation approved by the Assembly. It also urged church consideration of women in other positions of leadership.

The Lay Men

Lay men were never as well organized as the women. Christian Men's Fellowship groups were in most congregations but few had the vitality of those of the other gender. Still, when Wayne A.

Greene succeeded William H. McKinney upon McKinney's retirement as executive secretary of the Department of Men's Work in Indianapolis July 1, 1964, there were 100 men's weekend retreats annually involving some 10,000 men.

A decade later, seeking to capitalize on the success of the Quadrennial for women, the men instituted what they called "Sessions" as an international men's gathering. The first was in 1976, with great success, though more modest in numbers than the women's gatherings. By that time, Elby Boosinger had succeeded Wayne Green as the staff executive. Sessions '76 for men was held at Purdue and drew 1,646 (of which 391 were ministers). Planners for the June 18-22 Sessions '76 engineered a coup by arranging for Jimmy Carter as a speaker who, when invited, was simply an appealing Baptist layman and former governor of Georgia. By the time of the Sessions he was a national political phenomenon not five months away from election as President of the United States.

More than half of the participants filled out evaluations after Sessions '76 and 97 percent of those urged the men of the church to have additional "Sessions." The Disciples' men did just that in 1979 and again in 1984. The gatherings continued enthusiastic but drew much smaller participation. Each of the latter two involved a few over 800 participants. Among the general projects in which the lay organization involved itself were scholarships for black ministerial students, raising nearly $100,000 over the decade of the 1970s, and the planting of trees in the expanding desert areas of the third world. The latter covered more than 1,000 acres of trees to be used for shelter, firewood, and erosion resistance.

Critics of the church's activism in the 1960s and its speaking out on social issues during the quarter century of the searching years often ascribed the loss of membership in the mainstream Protestant churches, the Disciples among them, to the lay people "voting with their feet" against such involvements by the church. Though church leadership often worried that social involvements might in fact be scaring membership away, studies in both the 1970s and the 1980s proved that it was not so. In fact, a major North American study in 1971 indicated that it was a clergy misreading of lay people that speculated there was great concern over the church's social involvements.

Studies on Social Involvements

That study, supported by 21 denominations in the United States and Canada, involved 3,454 interviews of church people averaging an hour and a half each. The scientific sampling was double the size used ordinarily by the professional pollsters for a national study. It "punctured preconceptions" right and left and its findings were written up in a book by that name by Douglas W. Johnson, a religious researcher, and George W. Cornell, the Associated Press religion editor.

Among those surprising findings were these: Lay people have fewer anxieties than clergy about speaking out on social issues and supporting ethnic minority causes. Practically no lay people withhold funds because their church has supported controversial issues and most of them disapprove of such tactics. (Lay people did report they wanted greater say in how funds are spent.) Lay people are more supportive of ecumenical activity than pastors. A strong majority of lay people are supportive of their national church bodies.

More than 70 percent of lay people feel their denominations should speak out on current social issues such as civil rights, the war and other pressing problems. More than 70 percent felt denominations should support minority groups in obtaining open housing and upgraded employment (though a large majority objected to giving money to groups with no strings attached). Lay people's participation in the church declines, the study showed, because of the pressure of time and other more compelling interests.

The findings were borne out in 1984 and 1985 by research undertaken relative to the so-called Electronic Church on television and by focus groups dealing specifically with the Christian Church (Disciples of Christ). The Electronic Church studies indicated that mainstream Protestant churches are not losing members to the television evangelists; instead, increases of support to the Electronic Church are accompanied by similar increases in support to mainstream religion. Further, the television church viewers, almost all of whom already are church members, trust their denominations and the leadership.

The Disciples of Christ Office of Communication underwrote focus groups studies in the urban Disciples stronghold of Dallas,

123

Texas, and in the less urban community of Hannibal, Missouri. Disciples in those groups indicated strongly they support their church and its leadership. Lay Disciples of Christ are disturbed about the church's decrease in numbers but they do not want to change its basic approaches to ministry. They definitely do not want it to adopt the flair and flamboyance in ministry of the television evangelists. It should be remembered that the research was taken before the TV evangelist scandals.

* * *

"Stories of . . . exemplary individuals are an important part of the tradition that is so central to a community of memory."

She was pure Arkansas and she loved being it. Even though some church leaders winced because they thought it beneath her dignity when she let loose with her Arkansas Razorbacks football yell—"Whooooooooo, pigs!"—the people in the pews saw JEAN WOOLFOLK as someone truly authentic, someone they could trust and adore. No starry-eyed theologian here. Yet, there was no question about her credentials and stature in the church.

She was a lawyer, an insurance executive, and a chartered life underwriter. President of the Arkansas Christian Churches. A newspaper's Arkansas Woman of the Year in 1973. The first woman Moderator of the Christian Church (Disciples of Christ). The first woman president of a general administrative unit of the Disciples. A Disciples representative to the World Council of Churches conference on sexism in Berlin in 1974 and the Council's General Assembly in Nairobi, Kenya, in 1975. She would be named 1978 Churchwoman of the Year by Religious Heritage of America. She would serve as a member of the central committee of the World Council of Churches. She would be awarded five honorary degrees.

But always she would be—Jean Woolfolk. She often carried a purse that was a University of Arkansas football helmet, the strap being the helmet face-guard. Everywhere she spoke—and she spoke hundreds of times—the last question from the audience would be "Would you call the hogs?" She always obliged, in her naturally gravelly voice with a volume that shook the rafters and brought delight to almost everyone. (She was a choir director and,

124

when she sang, the gravelly voice became a beautiful silky alto.)

At the San Antonio General Assembly in 1975, when she served as Moderator, the Disciples were called upon to vote on the Consultation on Church Union's "mutual recognition of membership"—which pledged denominations to work toward recognizing members of each other's churches as members of their own. The Disciples voted affirmatively, as did all the other denominations related to COCU, and the general secretary of COCU, Dr. Gerald F. Moede, who was present, was invited to come to a microphone to speak following the vote.

The Disciples had a three-minute time limit on speeches, measured by an electronic clock (borrowed from basketball) that counted down the last 30 seconds before the microphone abruptly shut off. When Moede began to speak the clock was activated. As he described the significance of recognizing each other as part of the same church the time expired and his microphone went dead. Said Woolfolk from the platform: "Jerry, that just shows how much you are now one of us!"

Born January 3, 1921, in Little Rock, she has lived there all her life, earning a Bachelor's degree in business administration from the University of Arkansas, Fayetteville, and a Doctorate in law from Arkansas Law School, Little Rock. She worked for 20 years at American Foundation Life Insurance, becoming senior vice president in 1974. She was called to the position of president of the Disciples Church Finance Council in 1976 to succeed Spencer P. Austin, who had led the church's fund-raising arm through the latter part of its Unified Promotion days. She was the lone woman on the church's 16-member General Cabinet. The call to the staff position came soon after she finished her 1973-75 term as the first woman Moderator of the Disciples.

Woolfolk served the finance council until January 31, 1983, when she retired. During the period the finance arm's total fund-raising efforts grew from $17.5 million per year to $26.3 million. She wrote—like she talked—in a folksy style that included use of her great-great niece Wendy in promotional pieces, a "Perk up your giving" campaign with a cup of coffee as a symbol, and "second-mile" program to encourage above-and-beyond giving by earmarking the extra to specific causes of the giving congregation's choice.

Because of her lay background, her intimate involvement with

125

what was going on, and her self-assuredness, Woolfolk was power-fully persuasive in the field. In a flier produced by the church, Jean Woolfolk answered the question: Why doesn't the church stick to preaching the gospel and keep out of social issues? Her reply was: "There is no way the church can do that. Social issues are what the gospel is all about. The gospel is good news—good news about people's relationship to each other and people's rela-tionship to God. The two go together. Jesus summed up the whole of the law in 'Love God and love your neighbor.' And when you start really caring about the well-being of your neigh-bor, you can't help but be involved in social issues."

She further elaborated on her philosophy about the church and its public witness. "The church has an obligation to do the best job it can of trying to determine that which is right, that which is in accord with the will of God. Then it uses that will as a plumb line which is held up to our social, our political, our economic institutions, saying, 'As we see it, this is what God says is right!' You cannot avoid making a judgment on the basis of saying, 'Well, some people disagree.' I think that making no deci-sion is, in fact, making a decision. The church is not fallible. It can err. But the church must act. Did the prophets and the great saints of the New Testament stop speaking the truth because they were afraid people might not agree?

"One cannot ignore the judgment of a majority of several thou-sand people, even if they are not the whole 1.2 million people (in the Christian Church). You might be surprised at the number of letters the church receives from the recipients of resolutions, and our actions have been the subject of debate in the halls of Con-gress. Personally, I have found the representative bodies of the church right far more often than wrong. I am convinced that Jesus Christ is present when two or three thousand are gathered in his name and that the church has a responsibility to speak out as his instrument."

Jean Woolfolk was never one to mince words.

9

Identity Through Social Witness

1976—*Lockheed accused of overseas bribes* (Feb. 4) . . . Friendship
Mission raided in Paraguay (April 10) . . . *Spain elections put all
western Europe under democracy* (June) . . . Jean Woolfolk 1st
woman general unit head (June 12) . . . General Board approves
covenantal relationship with colleges, funding formula (June 16) . . .
Men's Sessions 76 (June 18-22) . . . *Supreme Court OKs death
penalty* (July 3) . . . *U.S. Bicentennial celebration* (July 4) . . .
Legionnaires disease kills 29 in Philadelphia (July 21-24) . . . Moak
leads fraternal visit to Africa . . . *Carter elected* (Nov. 2) . . . *Mao
and Chou die, Gang of Four arrested.*

1977—*1st Episcopal woman ordained* (Jan.1) . . . *10,000 draft
evaders pardoned* (Jan. 27) . . . *Laetrile useless as cancer cure* (June
15) . . . General Board pressures Illinois on equal rights amendment
. . . Higher education institutions sign church covenant . . . Reconciliation celebrates 10th . . . *Bert Lance resigns Carter cabinet* (Sept.
21) . . . *Nuclear proliferation pact signed* (Sept. 21) . . . Kansas City
Assembly approves civil liberties for homosexuals (Oct. 21-26) . . .
South Africa absolves government of Biko death (Dec. 2).

With tears in her eyes and voice cracking, the Idaho homemaker read the deeply personal and tender letter from her son to
thousands gathered around her at General Assembly: "It is very
important you as parents not feel guilty because I, your son, am a
homosexual. Guilt implies fault, and fault implies a misdeed, and
I cannot consider myself a mistake . . . If your morality would
condemn me, first consider these things: I did not choose to be a
homosexual . . . the morality that could condemn me for something over which I have no control must itself be without
humaneness."

There have been few moments as dramatic, as emotional in
the public life of the Christian Church (Disciples of Christ). The
attendance at that 1977 General Assembly was the third largest
ever for a general convention of the Disciples of Christ—more
than 11,000. Some who heard Carol Blakley that day were further

127

angered in their opposition to the church's showing special consideration to a group they believed was trampling underfoot the morals of society. But most were impressed by the sincerity of a mother's plea and the difficulty of her decision to share it.

There was a burst of applause following the reading of the letter. The Assembly voted nearly two to one to call on society to pay special attention to protecting the civil liberties of what had come to be called "gays," in itself an offensive perversion of a word to many people.

The adopted resolution, "while neither approving of nor condemning homosexuality," urged "the passage of legislation on local, state and national levels which will end the denial of civil rights and the violation of civil liberties for reasons of sexual orientation or preference," and it called upon church members to advocate and support the passage of such legislation. The resolution took note of unfair application of the laws to homosexuals and decried their loss of jobs, homes, custody of children, credit, insurance, and licensing.

Perhaps the Blakley letter carried the issue, perhaps it did not. But clearly the issue of the church's response to the new openness of homosexual persons dominated that General Assembly. The amount of time devoted to business at the Kansas City Assembly was a record 22 1/2 hours (generally there are 17 or 18). More than a quarter of the business time was devoted to debate on the homosexual issue, much of it in parliamentary wrangling. Generally, there has been only one, perhaps two, counted votes at an entire Assembly. On the homosexual issue alone at Kansas City there were three. With 5,554 registered voters, it involved roughly 20 minutes each time a vote count had to be taken. A resolution condemning outright the homosexual lifestyle was defeated 2,304 to 1,538. An attempt to prevent dealing with a study paper on the subject was beaten 2,309 to 1,596. The civil liberties vote was 2,541 yes and 1,312 no.

Few people on either side of the question think of the 1977 Assembly in Kansas City as something other than a moment of anger and conflict tearing at the fabric of the nine-year-old restructured church. Twice the General Minister and President, Kenneth L. Teegarden, came down from the platform in midsession to weep—once by himself in the semi-darkness on the stairs alongside the stage; the other to attempt to reconcile a

Georgia lay person who vowed from the floor he would persuade his congregation to withdraw from the church over the issue.

There were powerful counter-calls: for the church to express its biblical mandate to love the unloved; and, for the church to heed the biblical admonitions against the abomination of homosexuality. All the while, the names of the great saints of the church and the world looked down from the balcony railing ringing the auditorium—that same railing which nine years earlier bore the shields "We Rejoice in God." The names were those of people who demonstrated the empowerment of love in their lives—Martin Luther King, Jr., Mother Theresa, Mae Yoho Ward, A. L. Shelton (Disciples doctor murdered by bandits in Tibet), to name a few. A student took the floor to point out the irony that the Assembly theme art, the Sistine Chapel hand of God reaching out to touch humanity, was painted by a homosexual, Michelangelo.

Homosexual Study Paper Rouses Ire

Much of the anger focused on a document that wasn't even intended for approval. While Disciples acted favorably on protecting civil liberties of homosexuals and turned down a resolution condemning homosexuality as a life style—saying Christians don't have all the answers on this "complex matter"—they offered only for study a controversial 8,000-word document on "Homosexuality and the Church." They referred to the Task Force on the Ministry the question of ordination of homosexual persons, a referral that two years later brought back a tactfully-worded answer commending existing regional procedures for assessing the qualifications of all ministerial candidates and adding that "recent studies have not convinced us nor the Church at large that the ordaining of persons who engage in homosexual practices is in accord with God's will for the Church."

The problem on the study document, and indeed on the entire issue, was that those who most feared that gay rights activism was threatening the North American family didn't want the church discussing the matter at all, unless it was to condemn homosexuals outright. Four Indianapolis ministers wrote to the General Minister and President prior to the General Assembly urging him to remove the homosexual items from the docket. In their concern that the discussion itself would be disruptive to the church, they overlooked the fact that for the General Minister and President to be able to short-circuit items properly filed for business by congregations, regions and general units would be to afford that officer more power than Disciples ever envisioned in restructure.

The Homosexuality and the Church study paper, according to its opponents, was biased in favor of a liberal position. In approving the paper for study, the Assembly made it clear that the majority believed homosexuality was a subject that Christians could not simply avoid. The paper was the result of an 18-month study by the Division of Homeland Ministries' task force on family life and human sexuality. It raised questions about the origins and interpretations of the eleven biblical references to homosexuality, saying that none of the references are in the life and teachings of Jesus. For Jesus, sin was in the breaking of relationships, the study said. The study went on to spell four possible options for the church: a rejecting-punitive stance, rejecting-nonpunitive, qualified acceptance, and full acceptance. Of the latter two, the first saw homosexuality not as a sin but a "perversion of the natural order" which preferably should result in abstention from sex, but, if not, at least "adult, faithfully committed relationships." The fourth option would affirm that same-sex relationships can express fully God's intention for human love and fulfillment—a position the framers of the study believed could not be justified under biblical injunctions against homosexual acts without "radical application."

General Board A Puzzle to Many

One of the church's problems that surfaced under the pressure of the 1977 General Assembly was the lack of trust in the General Board by some people—clearly a minority—and the lack of knowledge—perhaps more general—of what the Board was and what its purpose was. There was concern expressed on the Assembly floor of the possibility of manipulation of the homosexual issue by the Board. Some speakers indicated they thought the Board was made up of general staff and clergy, while, in truth staff at neither the general nor regional levels are permitted to be voting members of the board. Local pastors and lay people are almost its total makeup with the rules requiring that there be more lay people than pastors serving on it.

While one of the most difficult assemblies in terms of the intensity of the issues, it certainly was not the first in which

Disciples dealt with explosive questions. In fact, General Assemblies after restructure dealt with no more difficult social, economic, political and moral questions than the earlier International Conventions. Issues were very much the same and handled very much the same way before restructure and after.

The American psyche was at a low ebb in 1977. The repercussions of a war in Vietnam that had gone on interminably and then had been lost—57,000 American lives without an assurance that it was worth it—were more than people could deal with. Then came the realization that oil and other resources might be finite and controlled by foreign governments only too willing to choke it off to see the United States squirm. On top of that: the gays—those people many felt were threatening their children, their families, their homes. The family was my family, and, as indicated in the Habits of the Heart study, an extension of the individualism that is so much a part of the American character. The traditional family was under attack in other ways: divorce, domestic violence, live-in arrangements outside marriage, deliberately childless couples. But Gay Rights was a target upon which it was easiest to focus wrath.

Witness in the Global Context

If Disciples' involvements with the civil rights movement in the 1960s had not gotten them deep into identification with the poor and oppressed, overseas missionary involvements had—which became another issue. It was apparent after one worked for a time with the very poor in the third world that help could be dispensed forever without the poor gaining even a modest share of the abundance of life, and that there were social forces that preferred it that way. The biblical witness placed Jesus clearly in identification with the poor and oppressed (Luke 4:18). And the illustration circulated popularly among Disciples as well as other Christians: you can give a hungry person a fish and tomorrow that person will be hungry again but you teach the person to fish and you've freed her or him from dependency for a lifetime. It was pointed out that Jesus gave no one alms but healed them instead, making them whole to go and live life more abundantly, liberated from dependence even on him.

Heeding this biblical understanding, most missionaries involved themselves in the life trials of those among whom they served in

131

the third world, helping people organize farm cooperatives, for instance, so they could reap more of the benefits of their own agriculture products. But organizing peasants or aboriginal populations for economic or political purposes threatens systems, profits and power. When those things are threatened, people in power often feel obliged to crush those who threaten them. When those things are threatened in places enveloped in the capitalist domain, people in power are apt to cry "communism." Therein lies trouble for missionaries who sincerely want to help all of God's children share in the abundance of God's world.

Missionaries Arrested in Work with Poor

Two Disciples missionaries in 1974 in the Philippines, Paul and Dede Wilson, quickly got themselves into trouble by their involvement with the urban desperately poor. They were not working outside channels. The executive of the National Council of Churches of the Philippines got into trouble with them. At a meeting in a home one night, the police of President Ferdinand Marcos, who was fighting a never-ending battle with the communists for control of the islands, raided and found a printing press (which wasn't allowed because of the possibility of printing anti-government materials) and a visitor who was on the wanted list. The Wilsons were incarcerated and for two weeks they and their 10-year-old son Jamie were held by the government. Finally they were released and ordered out of the country.

Two years later the police of dictator Alfredo Stroessner in Paraguay raided the Disciples' historic Friendship Mission, where the government said that work with the Indian peoples in community organization was in fact subversion. There was little question that as missionaries tried to help the people get better control of their economic situation those who were benefiting from their oppression were being discomfited. This in turn brought pressure to bear on the government to keep the peasants in their place. With the raiding of the mission, missionary Frisco Gilchrist, who had been working in the country for a quarter century, was arrested along with Ecuador's Victor Vaca, and held for a time before being expelled. Gilchrist was an unlikely appearing revolutionary—older, with a gentle manner and short military haircut.

Most Disciples could sympathize with North American missionaries and overseas nationals arrested under such circumstances.

But many could not. There was that gnawing concern among some people that if the missionaries were not doing something they shouldn't be, they wouldn't have been arrested. It was difficult for some to equate the contemporary incidents with the repeated arrests of the New Testament followers of Jesus. Yet, the circumstances were similar: witnessing that threatened political power, and service to the needy in a way that disrupted the economy. (The Philippian slave girl's owners dragged the apostles to the authorities when they realized their chances of making money were gone. The silversmith in Ephesus charged Christians were bad for business!)

A measure of good came from the arrests and expulsions of the Wilsons and Gilchrists. Paul Wilson and Frisco Gilchrist were engaged jointly by the Divisions of Homeland and Overseas Ministries to inaugurate American Christendom's first full-time staffed human rights office. Their task was to identify human rights infractions around the world and educate Disciples at all levels of church life to the evil embodied in officially sanctioned or tolerated injustices.

Issues Same Before, After Restructure

During the quarter century of the restructure period, 1960-1985, there were 17 international gatherings of the Disciples. Eight were "conventions," prior to restructure, most with voting by everyone who registered and attended. Nine were representative General Assemblies after the advent of restructure. In those eight pre-restructure conventions, Disciples dealt with 258 business items (in addition to the unit reports), an average of 32 per year, approving 82 percent of those acted upon.

Only once did the convention go against the advice of the Committee on Recommendations. The committee's task was to do the deeper exploration since a mass meeting of thousands hardly could be expected to intensively study the resolutions. The committee then made recommendations which, after the issues were debated on the floor, were voted upon by the whole body. The committee's work during those restructure-shaping years earned a 99.6 percent approval rate from the convention-goers. The one time a committee recommendation was overturned was in 1967 when the convention opposed support of conscientious objector status for people who objected to serving in the Vietnam

War but were not sure about making the claim for all wars. A year earlier Disciples in Assembly had said "yes" to the question—conscientious objectors to "particular" wars ought to be protected by law.

The measure, initiated by the Disciples Peace Fellowship, called attention to the "increasing number of young men in our Brotherhood and elsewhere (who) base their conscientious objection to war on the traditional Christian concept of a 'just war' but do not take the complete pacifist position of opposing all wars." The resolution cited the Nuremberg war crimes trials after World War II as establishing the crucial nature of individual conscience even in the face of orders from civilian or military authorities.

In 1967, military chaplain E. Tipton Carroll, Jr. appeared in his captain's uniform and argued powerfully against such a position as undermining the young men who make a conscious decision to defend their country. Carroll said there were "insidious programs" going on all over the U.S. to help men fail their Selective Service physical examinations. The nation was struggling with the issue of draft evaders fleeing to Canada by the thousands while other young men who obeyed the law and went to Vietnam risked or gave their lives. The Committee on Recommendations favored selective conscientious objection by a 98-76 vote. But the convention, moved by the debate, said "no" in a standing vote, with no count necessary.

The next year, 1968, the decision was reversed again. The resolution this time urged "the United States government to provide legal status and recourse for the conscientious objector to a particular war as is provided for the conscientious objector to all wars in forms of alternative services to one's country." It was signed by 42 leaders of the church, many of them related to higher education institutions and involved in counseling young people.

Russell Fuller, a Michigan pastor, argued that society offers ways to serve the country both for those who choose to fight and those who conscientiously object. "If a man cannot say for sure he would never fight, we give him three alternatives: to turn his back on his conscience, to become a felon, or to become a fugitive. The church of Jesus Christ must ask for something better." The vote was 1,725 in favor of selective conscientious objection, 845 against. The count took twelve minutes with tellers scattered among the seating sections. It was another first for the Disciples—

the first counted vote as a representative assembly. There were no vote counts in 1967 at the first delegate assembly.

Approval Rate Slips Slightly

After restructure, the representative General Assembly continued to support the wisdom of the 250-member General Board, though the approval percentage slipped a bit. As might be expected, the volume of business at General Assemblies almost doubled since the gathering no longer was annual but biennial. There were 453 business items on the dockets of the nine Assemblies from 1969 through 1985, an average of 50 per Assembly. The General Assembly adopted 83 percent of the items filed, a single point higher than the pre-restructure adoption rate. Six times during that post-restructure period the Assembly took the opposite action of what was proposed by the General Board, an approval rate of 96.7 percent.

On nine other occasions the Assembly declined to follow the specific recommendations, largely showing an unwillingness to refer matters for further study when they could be approved outright. One of the six reversals of General Board recommendations constituted a warning to the General Board not to overstep its bounds. The Assembly in 1973 defeated a measure that would have permitted the General Board to speak on new subjects "in its own name" between Assemblies.

The positions of the gathered Disciples on issues remained quite similar after restructure to those held prior to it. Before restructure, the convention's business items were about 28 percent in the realm of what could be called public social witness. Nearly 11 percent were related to matters of structure. The remainder was split roughly between actions having to do with operational decisions and matters of internal witness. After restructure, the structural matters declined to 4 percent of the total business and the public witness items went up to 35 percent. Between 1975 and 1985 questions of structure consumed only 1.4 percent of the church's business docket.

The Disciples regularly opposed the death penalty, both in the pre-restructure days when the United States Supreme Court was ruling it unconstitutional and in the mid-1980s when the Court was reversing itself. Disciples favored gun control before and after reorganizing their deliberative processes. They called on the

United States to review its involvement in Vietnam during the convention days, urging amnesty for the draft evaders and reconciliation with Vietnam after the war. They discouraged investments in South Africa in the 1960s and called for economic sanctions in the 1980s. Disciples strongly supported the Supreme Court bar to a state-authorized prayer in public schools in 1962 and apparently saw no reason to change that position when the issue arose again in the early 1980s.

They spoke out on behalf of the elderly, on low-income housing, both before and after, and on world hunger. Disciples pleaded for a halt in the nuclear arms race in 1962, again in 1985. They called for seating China in the United Nations in 1964 (by a 897 to 655 vote) when the idea was anathema to many Americans, China being seated seven years later with U.S. government support; the Disciples urged in 1977 full diplomatic relations with China, a move the United States subsequently made. Generally with respect to other nations, the Disciples consistently favored humanitarian support and opposed military aid. Before restructure, Disciples acknowledged the use of non-violent civil disobedience as a last resort for Christians to right wrongs. In 1985, the Assembly cited non-violent civil disobedience as a means of resisting any move by the United States to escalate involvement in the civil war in Nicaragua.

Many Disciples Unaware of Issues

The Division of Homeland Ministries engaged a major research effort in 1985 that indicated the difficulty of congregations in treating controversial public issues. The DHM study cited the following percentages of survey respondents who didn't remember the issues ever being mentioned in their congregations: sanctuary movement (protecting illegal aliens), 55 percent; arms race, 57 percent; nuclear weapons, 57 percent; refugee resettlement, 66 percent (though Disciples as a body were among the most active churches in refugee resettlement); U.S. military interventions, 67 percent; civil disobedience, 68 percent; abortion, 71 percent; and homosexual rights, 72 percent. However, 78 percent of the respondents felt that the minister was placing the proper emphasis on the issues and about the same percentage felt she/he was providing enough opportunity for the airing of different views.

Corporate social responsibility was one of the issues that repeatedly cropped up among Disciples during the 1970s and 1980s. The United Christian Missionary Society, which continued to exist with a small board to manage its stock holdings, almost annually challenged one corporation or another on defense-related involvements, South Africa stocks, sexism or racism in management, or environmental despoiling. By action of the 1971 General Assembly a special task force on ethical investments developed guidelines for both church organizations and individual Christians to use in investing. The guidelines leaned toward seeking change through voting power rather than divestiture.

The Disciples joined in the lengthy 1980s boycott against Nestle because of the Swiss firm's baby formula marketing tactics in the third world which were believed to be endangering baby health. Finally, in January 1984, Nestle agreed to the World Health Organization guidelines. Rafael D. Pagan Jr., a Nestle executive, was invited to speak to the General Board. At the conclusion of the presentation, Disciples Moderator William E. Tucker pulled two Nestle's candy bars from his pocket, offered one to Pagan and the two of them shared the sweets publicly to the delight of the General Board.

* * *

"Stories of . . . exemplary individuals are an important part of the tradition that is so central to a community of memory."

An ordained Disciples of Christ minister, FRANK A. ROSE performed an unusual service. He reintegrated schools. School systems that in the mid-1970s had segregated again after the original struggles of the 1950s and 1960s. He was a consultant working with Ford Foundation money. He provided strategies for school leaders in dealing with the problems. His clients were among the biggest cities—Los Angeles, Dallas, Louisville.

Rose had earned his reputation during a confrontation of epic proportions back in 1963. He was the 43-year-old president then of the University of Alabama. His task was to enroll the first blacks there. The Kennedy brothers—President John F. and Attorney General Robert F.—were his allies. Governor George

Wallace, who vowed to block the entrance, and the Ku Klux Klan were his opponents.

Tuscaloosa was extremely tense that June. The hope was that somehow the University of Alabama might admit its first two black students without violence. But Tuscaloosa was Klan territory. National Klan leader Robert Shelton lived there. An attempt to enroll Autherine Lucey seven years earlier had ended with cars being overturned and the Klan frightening the young woman and her supporters away. Now cross burnings around the campus were a regular occurrence. Threatening phone calls to university leaders were routine. Thirty-two people had been killed in Alabama since civil rights pressure began. Two men from New Jersey had been arrested in town only two weeks earlier with sticks of dynamite.

However, in the previous October, James Meredith had successfully become the first black student at the University of Mississippi, though not without riots and 2,000 troops to quell them. Now it was Alabama's turn. Two young, carefully chosen blacks from a pool compiled by Martin Luther King Jr., were to enroll officially June 6. Federal marshals were on campus to enforce the order to integrate. Gov. Wallace, who had arrived the night before, had a force of state troopers with him. News media from all over the world, including the Soviet Union, were on hand.

Rose, distinguished looking, dark-haired, was a son of the South, born in Mississippi not 30 miles from where in 1964 law officers would be involved in the disappearance and murder of three civil rights workers. Rose had been recruited as university president because he was committed to racial integration. While outsiders saw Alabama through the media as a place of Wallaces and "Bull" Connors, fire hoses and police dogs, fiery crosses and white hoods, many of the distinguished citizens of the state were embarrassed by segregationist demagoguery and looked for ways to overcome it. The trustees of the university were among them.

Rose was 34 years old and the president of Transylvania University in Kentucky when the 1954 Supreme Court decision overruled the separate-but-equal notion of public education. Rose was called by the Kentucky governor to help plan racial integration in the state. The college administrator spoke about that experience at a national fraternity convention in Florida in 1957 and was invited to speak about it again at a banquet of the University of Alabama trustees. He was impressive.

Soon thereafter Rose was offered the University of Alabama presidency but he said he was committed to small college liberal arts education and wasn't interested. The 84-year-old chairman of the trustees appealed to the talented Southerner's conscience: "If we can't count on our young men coming back to help solve the problems. . . ." In 1957 Rose accepted the challenge, leaving the Disciples-related college he had headed since he was 30 years old.

It was spring 1963 when the moment finally came. Frank Rose was perched in a second floor window in the athletic office building across the quadrangle from the gymnasium where university students were registering for the summer term. It had been a tough few months. Rose was required to have a policeman with him whenever he left his home. Even at the airport, the university's plane and pilot were required to go aboard for 30 minutes before Rose could board—just to avoid any possible aircraft tampering by the KKK.

The strategy on June 6 was to keep everybody, including the university administration, away from the confrontation site as best as possible. So Rose was with the other trustees plus the editors of several national news magazines in a window across the way. Rose had been up most of the night on the telephone with the Kennedys. The President tried to talk the university out of going through with the integration attempt at that moment. He was in the midst of negotiating with the Soviet Union to get Bay of Pigs invasion prisoners out of Cuba and he didn't want a domestic crisis. But Rose insisted there was no turning back. The telephone calls between the university president and Washington were placed from a pay phone on the highway toward Birmingham since even the Army Signal Corps, which had set up phones in the president's mansion, could not avoid the KKK's wiretap.

Across the way, the governor and his entourage were waiting the arrival of the students. At the appointed hour of 9:30 a.m., deputy attorney general Nicholas Katzenbach led the two students by hand, a young man on one side and a young woman on the other, to the gymnasium entrance. The students had been given scholarships by the university and had been admitted to university housing earlier. "I've come to enroll the students. Please step aside, governor," said Katzenbach. Wallace replied: "I'm going to make my statement." Then Wallace read his statement about the sovereignty of the state of Alabama over its education. He continued to block the entrance. "Step aside, governor," said the deputy attorney general. Nothing happened. "I'm under the orders of the President to come with the two students and enroll them," Katzenbach said. Still no movement. Katzenbach then retreated, taking the two students back to their dormitory to wait the next move.

By prearrangement the U.S. would federalize the National Guard and attempt again at 3:00 p.m. to enroll the students. After lunch the napping Rose was wakened by a call from President Kennedy who had withdrawn himself from international crises long enough to find out what was going on in Alabama. Rose asked the President if the Guard would be in a position to arrest the governor. No, Kennedy replied, that would be the worst thing to do. "What then?" asked Rose, "We're going to have to play it tough." The President felt that since the governor had made his stand, he might be satisfied without pressing to the inevitable conflict. He was right. When 3:00 p.m. came the governor was gone. Later Gov. Wallace called Rose from the airport and expressed appreciation to him for a well-handled integration without violence. An hour after that President Kennedy was on the phone with similar congratulations.

Frank Rose was born in Meridian, Mississippi, in 1920. He earned his Bachelor of Arts degree at Transylvania, in Lexington, and followed that with a Bachelor of Divinity from Lexington Theological Seminary. At 27 he became a professor of philosophy at Transylvania, three years later the institution's president.

In September, 1969, Rose left the University of Alabama for a post as chairman of the board of the General Computing Corporation and president of its affiliated education, health and research foundation, University Associates. His work evolved into that of a promoter of support for struggling black colleges and institutions for children's health care. In 1974, he was called upon to help reintegrate the Louisville schools. Though suffering health problems, Rose in the 1980s was raising support for some 20 medical centers engaged in children's health and infant mortality programs, as well as writing legislative language for congressional action on civil rights, black colleges, children's health and nutrition and infant mortality.

10

An Aberration Within

1978—*Italy's Moro kidnapped, murdered* (March 16) . . . *Carter shelves neutron bomb* (April 7) . . . *Senate votes to turn over Panama Canal* (April 18) . . . Sixth CWF Quadrennial draws record 4,914 women (June 26-30) . . . *Bakke case ends racial quotas* (June 28) . . . *First outside womb baby fertilization* (July 26) . . . *Camp David accords between Israel, Egypt signed* (Sept. 17) . . . *Poland's John Paul II new pope* (Oct. 16) . . . *People's Temple mass suicide in Guyana* (Nov. 18) . . . *U.S., China open diplomatic relations.*

1979—*Kampuchea's Pol Pot falls* (Jan. 7) . . . *Shah flees Iran after year of upheaval* (Jan. 16) . . . Disciples say no to controls to prevent Jim Jones situations (March 11-13) . . . *Thatcher wins in Britain* (March 28) . . . *Three Mile Island leaks* (March 28) . . . Men hold Sessions 79 (June 11-15) . . . *Carter, Brezhnev sign Salt II* (June 14) . . . *Somoza flees Nicaragua* (July 17) . . . *Pope visits U.S.* (Sept. 29-Oct. 7). . . Disciples Ecumenical Council meets in Jamaica (Oct. 7-12) . . . *Korea's Park assassinated* (Oct. 26) . . . *Federal $1.5 billion loan to Chrysler* (Nov. 1) . . . *U.S. embassy seized in Iran* (Nov. 3) . . . *USSR invades Afghanistan* (Dec. 27).

When one of history's great tragedies began to unfold on television and newspaper front pages November 19, 1978, some Disciples of Christ in Indiana and California went into immediate shock. Soon Disciples all over North America would recoil in horror as they saw the denomination's name on network television nightly. The murder-suicide of 918 people including a California Congressman in South America was the work of a pastor and congregation affiliated with the Christian Church (Disciples of Christ)! Peoples Temple had begun its bizarre odyssey in Indianapolis in 1960 when it affiliated with the Disciples. Pastor Jim Jones had been ordained by the Disciples of Christ February 16, 1964, in the same city.

When California Congressman Leo Ryan, accompanied by newsmen, decided to fly to Guyana and investigate reports that members of a California church were being held against their will at a community carved out of the jungle and called "Jonestown," he triggered a holocaust that the Gallup Poll found to be the biggest news story since the atomic bombing of Hiroshima. The Congressman and his party flew to a small airstrip a few miles from the Jones settlement.

Ryan found the situation tense in Jonestown, although he was welcomed cordially and escorted about for two days. He was shown the housing and the fields and recreation facilities of this isolated "agricultural project" that had been building for four years. As Ryan and his party began to leave, a few members of the church sought to leave with him and then others made efforts to secure seats on the small plane. As the visitors drove to their plane with two of the defectors, they were followed by a truck. While the Congressman and party were preparing to board the plane, Jones' camp guards opened fire from the truck, killing Ryan, a defector and three newsmen, including a cameraman who filmed the prelude to his own death.

Meanwhile, Jones, a strangely captivating preacher and faith healer whose paranoia may have been stimulated with drugs and drink, began having his camp nurses and doctors prepare a vat of cyanide-tainted fruit drink, knowing that the deaths at the airport would bring down on his head a society from which he was trying to escape with his followers. This mass suicide he termed a "revolutionary act." His flock had practiced it many times before, probably never fully comprehending the meaning of the rehearsal. Parents began giving paper cups of the drink to their children— not without protest but they were too dependent upon Jones to resist—and drinking the potion themselves. The horrible event was tape recorded and on the recording Jones was heard exhorting the people over the camp public address system to keep their children from screaming and to do what had to be done. Jones killed himself with a pistol apparently after all the others were dead. Only a sick woman unnoticed in a hut and two or three guards who fled through the forest escaped.

"Never Betray Your Trust and Confidence"

James W. Jones, born in rural Indiana May 13, 1931, appeared before the Indiana Disciples' commission on the ministry on January 28, 1964, and requested ordination. He told the commission: "I feel that Christ's teachings of universal love and

142

yet a positive program for overcoming evil by non-violent means affords the ultimate and ideal philosophy for all times." He called himself a strong proponent of applied Christianity, his primary concern as a minister being the "social problems of our age, such as poverty, war, racialism, and extreme nationalism."

He said he was proud to be a Disciple. "I have never once witnessed a fellowship which offers such latitude on the non-essential issues and still maintains such a tremendous dedication to resolving the important personal and collective needs of today." He commented how "non-typical" his Peoples Temple was and praised Disciples for their "complete empathy and understanding." He concluded his short presentation with: "If you will be so kind and considerate to grant me ordination I assure you that I will never betray your trust and confidence."

He seemed to be performing a significant interracial ministry, feeding the poor and working with the down-and-out blacks of the city. The city of Indianapolis had him on its human rights commission and his work was applauded. And so on February 16 at 8:00 p.m. there was a service of ordination at Peoples Temple Christian Church. It followed the usual pattern. The chairman of the ordaining council said to the presiding minister, "Sir, it is my happy privilege to report that the council has carefully studied the credentials of James Warren Jones, investigated his preparation and his life, and questioned him thoroughly as to his intent and purpose and we do now present him for ordination into the ministry of the church."

The presiding minister (from Jones' own congregation) told Jones the ministry is a high calling, not to be entered into lightly and asked him if he were willing to consecrate his life and talents. Presumably Jones said, "yes." The ordination program doesn't include the response. Then the presiding minister asked the participants: "Do you accept James Warren Jones . . . pledging the love, esteem, cooperation and fellowship of the church to him insofar as his life and labors shall continue to merit these?"

In 1965, Jones' near downtown Indianapolis congregation numbered about 230 members. But a year later the congregation was gone from Indiana. Jones had moved to California and to the amazement of the Indianapolis community nearly a hundred members of his congregation went with him. He complained about Indianapolis not being receptive to interracial living. A peaceful, secluded valley in California would provide a haven from the American racial conflict to come.

Jones planted Peoples Temple in Redwood Valley, near Ukiah and on the edge of the Mendocino National Forest 130 miles north of San Francisco. Jones re-related the congregation to the Disciples of Christ, California North region. The church's membership, largely black, numbered 86 that first year in California. The numbers reported by the Temple grew gradually, but impressively, until 1971 when they suddenly tripled and 1973 when a Los Angeles "branch" of the Temple opened, also carrying Jones' name as the pastor and counting almost as many members as the mother church. The reported membership of Peoples Temple leaped from 722 in 1970 to 2,203 the next year. In 1973 there were 2,814 members in Redwood Valley and 2,526 in the new Peoples Temple of Los Angeles. By the time the end came, Peoples Temple claimed to have 3,364 members in Northern California and 2,895 in Los Angeles. Whether those figures were intended to include the nearly 1,000 in Jonestown, Guayana, is not clear.

The church's growth and wealth became legend. Jones and his wife adopted children of different races and the picture was one of sacrificial life for others. The church hired lawyers and publicists and overblown publications abounded, telling of the healings and ministries of Jones and the Temple. The Temple constantly was in the public eye, demonstrating for one cause or another or honoring a legislator or public figure. A number of intellectuals and professional people associated themselves with the congregation, many becoming what appeared to be volunteer staff.

Peoples Temple also reported large amounts of money given to causes related to the Disciples of Christ—including some $200,000 the final year of its life—but almost all of it was designated to capital projects, ecumenical involvements and race and poverty-type ministries handled directly by the Temple. "Disciples-related" contribution was interpreted broadly in Indianapolis. Its reporting was on the honor system.

In 1972, Jones and the Temple had caught the eye of the *San Francisco Examiner* newspaper. A reporter attended some of the healings and wrote that Jones was faking miracle cures, taking the life savings of the elderly to operate the Temple, stationing armed guards at services, currying favor with public officials, and even involved in retaliatory break-ins against the newspaper. The charges sounded farfetched to Disciples, though admittedly few were familiar with the Temple. The *Indianapolis Star* followed up with stories of its own about Jones' alleged abuse of parishioners.

No Church Machinery to Probe Jones

Neither the regional office in Oakland nor the denominational headquarters in Indianapolis possessed the desire nor the machinery to begin "investigating" ministers and congregations. The charges had to do with criminal allegations and the state should handle that. Disciples had no background in this century for disciplining or defrocking ministers. The Disciples felt they embraced a variety of approaches to ministry on the basis that God makes the final judgment as to validity. Putting humans too much in the position of evaluation and judgment left the possibility of some worthy prophetic ministries being suppressed because they did not fit the "norm." Yet, how does a body of Christians protect itself from charlatans and worse? And when and how are they able to determine when a minister is a charlatan? Even restructure had not provided the means. Only months before the Jonestown tragedy—and related to a discussion of restructure—Ronald E. Osborn wrote in *Experiment in Liberty*: "The Christian Church (Disciples of Christ) . . . has no power to control the life of its congregations. A member, minister, or congregation can get out of the Christian Church almost too easily, but it is virtually impossible to 'throw out' any of those who want to stay."

In fact, the church's restructure design offers precise instructions how to withdraw, that being one of the guarantees made to assuage the opponents of restructure. There is no reference to actions by the body of Disciples of Christ to force a congregation out. That would have been a political impossibility in the drafting and passage of the restructure document. Opponents would have cited it as the evidence that restructurists intended to exercise tightfisted control over congregations.

The Disciples' General Minister and President, A. Dale Fiers, asked the church's general counsel, Wade D. Rubick, to visit the Temple while on other business in California more than five years before the tragedy. Temple officials, as part of their effusive public relations campaign, had offered to underwrite visits of denominational staff to California. Denominational leadership had not accepted, not because of any suspicions but because that was just

145

not the way things were done. Rubick, traveling on his own budget, did visit and saw nothing on the surface other than Jones' unusual charisma. The visit was not intended to be investigatory.

The Temple and Jones meanwhile continued to identify themselves with influential people and influential causes. They contributed to various local and national public service groups, including Religion in American Life (RIAL), a non-profit vehicle by which Christians and Jews advertised jointly in the mass media. When RIAL cited 100 ministers across the United States, including Jones, for their financial support of the program, the Temple's zealous followers typically exaggerated it in communications as naming Jones one of the top one hundred ministers in America.

Jones Initiates Guyana Community

In 1974 Jones built his "agricultural community" on the South American east coast between Venezuela and Brazil. He named it after himself and took his most dependent followers there to begin a new life. The Temple communities in California continued, helping to circulate brochures in the United States about the paradise of Jonestown, showing laughing children running and playing. The materials carried quotes from Jonestown residents about the joys of the communal life there. From time to time, defectors from the Temple in the United States raised ugly charges, about beatings and coercion.

Though the Temple continued to maintain a nominal relationship to the Disciples, the ties appeared later to have been window-dressing alone. The Disciples Division of Overseas Ministries rejected attempts by the Temple to relate the Jonestown work to the overseas missions of the denomination. It was learned after the tragedy that Jones used the Disciples name to impress the prime minister of Guyana and secure services or special treatment. He referred to himself as a "top leader" of the two million member denomination (exaggerating the size of the denomination to almost double) and implying he had the support of that many Christians.

The Disciples' Northern California regional commission on the ministry began to worry in 1977 that there might be truth to the accusations against him. The commission decided to confront him with the charges and review his standing as a minister in the region. It was the practice of the region not to make a review of standing without the person in question having an opportunity to make a response. But by that time Jones appeared to be hiding out in Guyana and the commission doubted he would return to face any questions. Not having any idea of the tragedy that was about to unfold, the commission let the matter rest for months, uncertain how to deal with it. Jones still had political clout with various state and local governments and even as the press carried the news of the deaths, invitations were arriving in San Francisco for a special Peoples Temple benefit with a popular state assemblyman presiding.

The first news reports from Guyana were sketchy. A Congressman and some newsmen had been killed while visiting a cult colony called Jonestown. Then reports of seeing bodies from the air—as many as 400—at Jonestown and the possibility of a mass suicide. Finally the grim fullness of the tragedy burst upon the world's conscience. As newsmen learned of the relationship of the Temple to the Disciples of Christ they began calling headquarters in Indianapolis. Kenneth Teegarden, the General Minister and President, acknowledged the Temple's ties to the Disciples and assured full cooperation to the news media.

Few Indianapolis leaders ever had met Jones so there was little information to share. Teegarden quickly vowed to raise with the Administrative Committee whether the church needed to tighten its procedures to deal with errant congregations and ministers. He had no intention of pressing for such action but, if any were to be taken, the Administrative Committee, which was meeting three months later, was the place. That move eased some of the hammering pressure from the media on the executive.

Tragedy Raises Ambiguities for Disciples

For the first few days, Disciples leaders received dozens of angry calls from church members, wondering why the Disciples could have allowed themselves to be associated with such a minister and congregation and asking how a disassociation could be made with the remaining elements of the Temple itself. Peoples Temple disbanded after the Jonestown massacre and that part of the question became moot. Also, the tone of the calls changed after those first few tumultuous days. As Disciples began to realize that control over congregations could mean control over "their" congregation, ambivalences arose. Most of the later calls expressed

147

the desire that leadership not over-react to the tragedy by trying to create some denominational authority over congregations.

The U.S. media, for the most part, soft-pedaled the tie between Peoples Temple and the denomination. It was obvious Jim Jones and the Temple were an aberration and this was the most shocking example of the degradation of religious cults, upon which the media had been directing their attention for some time. The *New York Times* went out of its way to describe the Disciples of Christ as "highly respected" at each initial mention of the name.

On March 11-13, 1979, the Administrative Committee met in Indianapolis. Upon Teegarden's recommendation, the Committee reaffirmed the church's commitment to the covenantal relationship between various elements of the church and to congregational freedom. "Rather than taking an action that would involve passing judgment on a congregation's ministry," the Administrative Committee resolved that the church "continue to develop new and creative ways for shepherding congregations and encouraging them to accept and live in a relationship of mutual support with other congregations in their region and the whole church; that the regions be encouraged to establish ways and means for at least annual visits to every congregation and to request all persons who hold ministerial standing to report annually on the ministry in which they are involved."

Further, said the Administrative Committee, the General Board's committee on ministerial standing needed to establish specific procedures to follow when a minister begins to function outside the country and without the sanction of denominational overseas operations. However great the temptation, the inclination was not to disturb the Disciples' basic understandings of the church and relationships of Christians to each other in attempting to correct a deviation that probably would have happened whatever the structure.

Counting the Costs to Disciples

What were the effects on Disciples of the Jonestown tragedy? It left leadership embarrassed, for one thing, that contact with a listed congregation could be so minimal that appropriate ministrations to the suffering survivors were not possible. It made clear that Disciples treasure their freedoms and wouldn't want to give them up even in the face of the most trying of horrors. It showed that the restructured church still has much to learn about developing appropriate relationships among general, regional and congregational expressions.

It indicated that while unique and different ministries are to be admired and encouraged, the church must face the fact that there are ministries that are exploitive, manipulative, degrading, and perhaps criminal—even in a mainline denomination. What does a free church like the Disciples of Christ do to deal with situations in which exploitation takes place?

While Jonestown might be written off as a once-in-a-millennium tragedy, does the church as a whole have an obligation to itself and society to evaluate and affirm—or disavow—the workings of its parts? Are there testing processes—should there be?—of ministers and their continued fitness to serve? (The regional commissions on the ministry do review standing on the basis of continued fitness.) What are the minimal contacts of a congregational oversight process and what constitutes oversight? (The Administrative Committee went only so far as to suggest the region should be in contact with each congregation at least once a year.)

The restructure of the church indicated that relationship to such a body as the Disciples of Christ involves both rights and responsibilities, then proceeded to identify and guarantee the rights. Should not the responsibilities be specified as well? Jonestown left many questions for which there were no answers forthcoming in the decade following.

Peoples Temple's name quickly disappeared from the denominational *Year Book and Directory*. Ironically, however, in the *Year Book* among a long list of names framed in a black border under the words "They rest from their labors . . . in loving memory of those who have served the church" was this entry: "Jones, James Warren—Jonestown, Guyana—November 18, 1978."

* * *

"Stories of . . . exemplary individuals are an important part of the tradition that is so central to a community of memory."

149

GRACE KIM, a second generation Japanese who had married a Korean, was back at work at Los Angeles' All Peoples Christian Center in 1978, her five children now grown and she anxious to earn a living as a divorcee and anxious to earn it through Christian service. Christians had inspired her when she was young and she was anxious to serve. As a teenager in 1942, she was one of the thousands of Japanese-Americans interned by the United States government during World War II. She lived for half a year in a horse stall at the Santa Anita racetrack and got her schooling in the grandstand.

What life had in store for her was leadership in her church. Trained in sociology and religion, Grace Kim returned to work at All Peoples (no connection with Peoples Temple, only an unfortunate name similarity) where she held her first job before settling at home to raise a family. She would be one of the national conveners of a new organization—American Asian Disciples. She would serve on the General Board of the Christian Church (Disciples of Christ). She would serve on social concerns and long-range planning bodies for the Disciples in the Pacific Southwest.

She would serve nationally on the Church Women's Coordinating Committee. She would be a member of the small committee that governs the Reconciliation race and poverty program of the church and determines which projects will receive some half a million dollars a year. She also would be on the committee that directs the program of Church Action for Safe and Just Communities. And she would represent her denomination in 1986 on a fact-finding and good will mission to Vietnam and Kampuchea.

Terminal Island in 1928 was the center of the Japanese fishing community near Long Beach, California. Grace Shiraishi was born there. Her father was the Baptist minister in the Japanese community. Like most preachers' kids she moved around a bit as father went to new assignments. To Pomona at age four, to Gardena at fourteen. And then an unanticipated move; two months after the Pearl Harbor bombing by the Japanese, the U.S. government served notice on Japanese-Americans they would be confined as security risks. They had about two months to dispose of their earthly goods.

At least one of her friends had a father that couldn't stand the humiliation. He committed suicide. Her first stop was the "assembly center" at Santa Anita racetrack, where there were watch towers and tanks and armed guards. The internees lived in the stables, and went to school in the grandstand. There were riots in camp. She can't remember the objective. Some of those interned could earn a little money making camouflage nets for the war effort. It seemed so incongruous. But not half as incongruous as, following three years of confinement in the permanent camp in southeast Arkansas, she and other teenagers parading to celebrate the American victory. They weren't allowed to have radios so she doesn't remember anything about atomic bombs being dropped.

The Arkansas camp was about the size of the city of Eureka, California. There she became acquainted with the Disciples of Christ for the first time. There were Disciples on the camp faculty. The state Christian Youth Fellowship invited camp young people to participate in events. At one of them she heard a great Disciples singer, Rosa Page Welch.

When the war was over, the family returned first to Los Angeles and then Gardena to pick up the pieces. She finished high school and then moved on to the University of Redlands, a Baptist school which went out of its way to befriend the Asians. She finished there and applied to the Los Angeles federation of churches for work. They found work for her in the fall of 1950 in child care at All Peoples.

All Peoples was an historic mission related to the Disciples of Christ, one originally known as Japanese Christian Institute. There still was a predominance of Japanese who came to the center for social services but there was a growing contingency of black, Hispanic and Caucasian. Grace married and left the center to raise her family. Her marriage to Don Kim ended in divorce. She is proud of her five children, one of whom is working as a nurse in an intensive care unit, another in psychology, and another in a drug abuse program.

When she returned to All Peoples in the mid-1970s, she began work with the Center's program of placing retired persons in volunteer service to hospitals, schools, service centers. Since few of the inner city volunteers would be educated or professional persons, most of the volunteer effort involves people who can do friendly visiting or telephone reassurance. But that could be the most important service offered to persons in need or confined.

All Peoples has a church connected with it. One of the men

who grew up in the church and the center is now a retired engineer. He is back as one of the senior volunteers. Grace Kim enjoys the "All Peoples" symbolism he represents. Aki Suzuki is Japanese. He teaches English as a second language to Hispanic children. And he teaches Spanish as a second language to black children.

11

Overseas Ministries:
A Maturing Identity

1980—*Abscam implicates officials* (Feb. 2) . . . Zaire, North American Disciples affirm ties at U.S. consultation (April) . . . *8 killed in Iran hostage rescue failure* (April 25) . . . *Mt. St. Helens erupts* (May 18) . . . 50th anniversary World Convention celebrated, Honolulu (July 15-20) . . . *U.S. boycotts Moscow Olympics* (July 19) . . . *Iraq invades Iran* (Sept. 19) . . . First general Edu-Care event (September) . . . *Reagan elected* (Nov. 4) . . . *Atlanta children missing* (Nov. 6) . . . *Nuns killed in El Salvador* (Dec. 4) . . . *John Lennon assassinated* (Dec. 8).

1981—Disciples resettle 1,100 refugees during year . . . *Iran hostages freed* (Jan. 18) . . . *Reagan wounded* (March 30) . . . *Space shuttle flight tested* (April 12) . . . *Belfast hunger strikers die* (May 5-July 13) . . . *Pope wounded* (May 14) . . . *O'Connor named to Supreme Court* (July 7) . . . *Kansas City Hyatt Regency disaster* (July 18) . . . *Charles, Diana marry* (July 29) . . . Anaheim Assembly adopts overseas philosophy (July 31-Aug. 5) . . . *Reagan fires air controllers* (Aug. 11) . . . British Disciples help form United Reformed Church (Sept. 26) . . . *Sadat assassinated* (Oct. 6) . . . *First test tube baby* (Dec. 28).

In three quarters of a century of missionary work in the Belgian Congo (Zaire), the Disciples of Christ of North America helped the church grow to 123,000 members, the largest overseas Disciples community in the world. But a new day dawned in the 1960s; the Zairians began administering their own church and the results were even more exciting. They quadrupled the numbers to more than half a million in one-third the time.

That illustration was a popular one in the 1980s as Disciples leadership attempted to show that the reduction in the number of overseas staff (missionaries) did not mean the church in North America was abandoning the preaching of the gospel overseas. In fact, it meant a maturing of the missionary concept and a loosen-

153

ing of the gospel of Jesus Christ from its "Western religion" taint.

There had been 83 missionaries in the Congo in 1960, the center of the church's mission activity worldwide. But in 1985 there were only 17. To some American and Canadian Disciples the decline represented a failure. But the results indicated otherwise. Zairians were baptizing 15,000 persons a year in 1985 when only 6,000 a year were being baptized a quarter century earlier.

In 1981, the Division of Overseas Ministries made what might be considered a daring move. The Division took to the whole church the philosophy of operation that had been building for more than half a century—in fact, was one of the excuses for breakaway by the Independent Christian churches in 1926-27. Legally, the Division could have kept the statement of policy confined to its board of directors. It was a deliberate move to validate—or, for that matter, invalidate—the division's operational philosophy through the authorized structures of the church. It also was to educate church people as to why mission was moving in the direction it was. It was one of the fruits of restructure; it demonstrated the wholeness of the church and accountability by its divisions of work.

When those General Principles and Policies of the Division of Overseas Ministries went to the General Assembly in Anaheim, California, July 31-August 5, 1981, they carried an introduction from Kenneth Teegarden, the church's General Minister and President: "The Principles and Policies are—first and foremost—thoroughly biblical. They are evangelical in the sense that they reach out to all peoples everywhere. They are radical in that they pursue a fundamental change in people. They offer a worldview that recognizes the Christian as servant, not master; the mission as losing one's self, not gaining. They will not be understood by everyone because the gospel is not of this world. They are our principles and policies, but they represent more of a challenge than a fulfillment. Which is as it should be."

The Disciples in Assembly overwhelmingly adopted the policies. They now were no longer the policies of the division. They were the policies of the church. They included commitment to working ecumenically overseas, to working as partners rather than masters of overseas churches, to identifying with the poor and oppressed. They were embodiment of what took place in the selfhood of the Zairian church as well as the Zairian nation and the blueprint for what was taking place in former missionary relationships all around the globe.

The Third Stage of Mission

Robert A. Thomas was fond of saying that there were three stages in the missionary history. The first was the planting stage, when the gospel seeds were being sown throughout the world. The second was the managing stage, in which missionaries from the West managed church institutions in third world countries. The third was the servant stage, in which First World churches demonstrated the servanthood that Christ took upon himself. Thomas, the president of the Division of Overseas Ministries, 1969-1983, declared that the first two stages were now past and that the third prevailed.

The Disciples were among the pioneers in encouraging self-administration by one-time mission churches abroad. In mid-1960 when the Belgian Congo received its independence, Disciples were ready to turn over the reins to the church that already was flourishing there. In Puerto Rico, missionaries essentially brought themselves home, saying there no longer was justification for the church in the U.S. and Canada to manage a church that was able and willing to think and act for itself. In most of Asia, Disciples already were relating to united and self-administering churches, some of which were forced into unity by Japanese military forces in the World War II era.

North American Disciples supported India Disciples when in 1970 they helped form the new united body called the Church of North India. Not all of these new relationships were received well by all North Americans. Some less ecumenically-inclined Disciples saw an opportunity for continued influence in India when a number of Disciples churches chose not to go into the united church. The North Americans provided some direct support and complained of abandonment of those congregations by Disciples.

The direction of Disciples overseas ministries had been a long progression toward partner rather than dominant relationships, toward ecumenical rather than sectarian witness, and to emphasis on the poor and the oppressed in addition to concern for "spiritual" needs. That direction followed the one taken by most mainline Protestant church denominations. The approach already was evident back near the turn of the century when more conservative

155

Christians complained that missionaries, particularly in China, were practicing "open membership," which meant that they were accepting Christians transferring into the churches who had not been immersed but baptized through other means. The missionary society denied it, but it was a point of tension nevertheless.

In Asia, World War II facilitated the direction. The Japanese government, in order better to keep an eye on Christians, forced them to unite. The direct result was the Kyodan, the United Church of Christ of Japan, which the Disciples and seven other denominations supported after the war as their partner church in Japan. There were united churches as well in the Philippines and Thailand, which Disciples helped create, and in Hong Kong to which they related.

Virgil A. Sly, for 25 years leading up to 1959, helped develop the policy of liberating the overseas churches, linking in partnership with them, working ecumenically and stressing human freedom. He was a major force for that position in the National Council of Churches. As chairman of foreign missions for the United Christian Missionary Society he was in the thick of the action and in the theorizing that brought the new mission day into being. Sly extended his influence in a term as vice-president of the National Council.

In 1959 the board of trustees of the UCMS put the "Strategy of World Mission" into a document that anticipated the 1981 policies. That document declared that "bread and land" are legitimate concerns of the gospel, that linkage of the gospel to the white race has been a handicap, and that the new day demanded an end to possessiveness of mission.

Involving the Whole Church

Robert Thomas had an enlightened vision of the wholeness of the church. He felt that the overseas policies ought not simply be the policies developed by staff and board of the Division of Overseas Ministries. If they in fact were to be the policies of the church, that expression of the total Disciples body that came out of restructure—the General Assembly—ought to be called upon to validate them. That was risky business. What if the General Assembly did not accept the ecumenical, partnership and social witness implications of the policy? The staff was so convinced that it was the will and the way of Jesus Christ they probably would have had to resign *en masse*!

The intensity of Disciples in their efforts to become a "church" and to do the will of Christ in a "churchly" manner ironically may have presented a stumbling block to more extensive ties of the overseas operations of the Disciples and their closest ecumenical partner, the United Church of Christ. Disciples and the United Church began administering their India work jointly March 1, 1967—Telfer Mook, a United Church India veteran, as the executive for both denominations. In September, 1968, they initiated a similar joint arrangement administering Latin America (an arrangement that ended December 31, 1971, due to differences in priorities).

A Difference in Philosophy

The Division of Overseas Ministries and the United Church Board for World Ministries held conversations in the 1970s about the possibility of linking all mission administration. The finding was that the overseas mission bodies of the two churches at that time were far apart in their understanding of the relationship of mission boards to their denominations. Disciples overseas staff and board, flush with the denomination having achieved what was felt to be a more "churchly" structure, had moved toward identifying their operations with the will of the General Assembly, as is evident by the 1981 policy validation.

The United Church Board for World Ministries, on the other hand, saw their role as one of an autonomous instrumentality able to be on the cutting edge of mission only as the persons with the most zeal and dedication for mission made the decisions. The difference in philosophy didn't keep the two churches from expanding joint administration. On May 1, 1980, the two established joint administration in the Middle East, with Dale L. Bishop as the executive, once again a highly successful venture, at least from the standpoint of Disciples.

When restructure came, the Overseas Ministries board and staff determined that there needed to be an updating of the 1959 mission strategy document but that it shouldn't be done until the new structure had a chance to "shake down." That took about four years. In 1976 Thomas encouraged the board and staff to begin rethinking the overseas role. A segment of each board meeting was turned over to that purpose. Thomas did the drafting but he had as a member of his staff Joseph M. Smith who had been the principal drafter of the 1959 strategy.

Joseph and Winifred Smith had been missionaries in the Far East when World War II broke out. They were imprisoned in the Philippines by the Japanese. In 1972 on the Asia fraternal visit, Joseph Smith met in Japan for the first time in 28 years the commandant of the prison in which he and Winifred were confined. It was at a Christian retreat center in Kyoto. The commandant, unlike the film depictions of the war, had befriended the Smiths and others.

At the Kyoto reunion, Dr. Smith shed a few tears, as did the other Americans present, when he described how the commandant, a non-Christian, was "a better Christian than I am." Then the two of them left the others, parted the sliding doors, and seated themselves on their knees, Japanese style, on the rice straw matting of the porch and in private exchanged gifts. It was one of the those moments that is unforgettable.

The General Principles and Policies, as finally produced, were very much the product of the board of the Division of Overseas Ministries. Thomas drafted and staff contributed, but over a four-year period the board shaped and corrected. General units of the church from the very beginning brought their financial and service reports to the General Assembly for review, and many brought special programs or projects to the Assembly for reflection and action, the Church Finance Council had brought its bylaws for approval, but the Overseas Ministries general philosophy statement was a first for the restructured church.

Faith Principles Undergird Overseas Policy

The General Board, which reviews on items going to the General Assembly, debated the overseas policy vigorously but made only a minor change and urged its approval. The policy, as adopted by the General Assembly of the Christian Church (Disciples of Christ) in Anaheim, includes 12 faith principles. In capsule form they are:

1. Mission is rooted in the scriptures, but always engaged in relation to the contemporary experience and context.
2. Missionary commitment is grounded in God's love for all humankind and Christ's liberating resurrection, expressing itself in

witness and service as well as engagement in "the struggle for a new and just community."

3. God has never, in any time or place, been without witness. (This was one of the most troubling yet exciting concepts in the policy. The implication is that God is present in such religions as Buddhism and Islam and may speak to Christians through them. Repeatedly the Bible recounts when God spoke and acted through people who were not of the Judeo-Christian faith—Cyrus of Persia, for instance, who brought the Hebrews out of Babylonian captivity and helped them rebuild the temple. Also, the concept is that the absence of Western Christians from a scene or the presence of severe persecution does not limit God. Presumably the resurgence of the Christian faith in China is an example of how God was working even when the Western church thought Christianity in communist China had vanished.)

4. The church is one, it exists for the sake of the world and not for itself, and its divisions are limitations on its proclaiming the good news and seeking the redemption of all humanity.

5. Accepting God's love, making a faith commitment and day-to-day decision-making involves Christians in the on-going process of the kingdom.

6. Discipleship makes Christians aware "they belong inescapably together" and enables a witness to the coming of the Kingdom.

7. The good news by its nature must be communicated.

8. The gospel always includes announcing God's love, the offer of grace, the invitation to repent, the summons to word and deed, responsibility in justice and human dignity struggles, the obligation to denounce all that hinders wholeness, and a commitment to the risk of life itself.

9. Christ calls the church to identify with the oppressed, the prisoners, the poor and the sick.

10. Social action and evangelism are one, proclamation of Jesus being incomplete without deeds.

11. Christ calls the church to stand against the "principalities" that oppress or destroy people.

12. Christ calls the church to support people who suffer on behalf of justice and freedom.

This approach to mission continued to mystify many Disciples who were weaned on traditional missionary concepts that envisioned "our" missionaries converting less civilized persons to the Christian faith. The policy helped North Americans recognize the achievements and acknowledge the dignity of the people in churches around the world. Sometimes it made it more difficult for North American Disciples to visualize their own role.

Missionaries to North America

The new approach began a minimal turn-about in missionary direction. The Minahasa church in Indonesia, with which Disciples are related, sent a missionary to Ohio and later another to Missouri. Puerto Rico sent missionaries to Miami. The Japanese church sent a missionary to Seattle. The new approach also was responsible for the organizing and dispatching of fraternal visits by the North America Disciples to Asia in 1972 and Africa in 1976. The concept was to relate common work in the United States to similar church work in the Asian countries or African countries, the object being to have the third world churches deal with a counterpart in the partner "church" and not simply a foreign mission executive. Moderator Walter D. Bingham led 24 executives to Asia for a month in 1972. Bingham and the others engaged in intimate dialogue at all levels and with all sorts of church and non-church people in Japan, Hong Kong, Thailand and India. In 1976 Moderator James A. Moak led a 19-member delegation to Liberia, Zaire, South Africa and Kenya.

On the 1972 trip, the delegation was riding the train from Tokyo to Osaka. An uproar commenced in the forward part of the passenger car. It lasted for half an hour and people were standing around, craning to see. Finally Division of Homeland Ministries executive Harold Johnson emerged from the midst, his new Japanese friends all smiles, waving and flashing "peace" signs to the Americans. Johnson, who had no Japanese language skills, had stopped while passing through the car when a young Japanese read aloud his name tag written in Japanese characters. Johnson, the epitome of a "people person," immediately began an exchange in which he attempted, singularly unsuccessfully, to learn some Japanese. His willingness to try, his lack of embarrassment and his obvious love and sincerity drew immediate admiration from the Japanese. Said Robert Thomas as Johnson returned to his seat, "Now, that is a missionary!"

Reaching More Than 70 Countries

When one includes the involvements around the world through the Week of Compassion, Disciples ended the restructure era with a regular annual outreach that touched more than 70 countries. Terms of four years or shorter became the standard for overseas staff (missionaries). The objective was to respond to requests from overseas for particular skills where they were most needed and continue the response only as the need continued. Some 20 percent of the overseas staff was ethnic minority by the end of the period, with a mix of assignments, such as a Paraguayan in Zaire.

While mission continued in such traditional Disciples locations as Zaire, India and Paraguay, Disciples were sending personnel to serve in the newer locations of Lesotho, Kenya, Nigeria, Swaziland, Ecuador, Indonesia and Singapore. They were in relationship with such Christian groups as the China Christian Council in Nanjing, the Pentecostal Church of Cuba, Evangelical Pentecostal Union of Venezuela, the Middle East Council of Churches in Beirut, and the Evangelical Committee for Help and Development in Nicaragua.

Including both the Division of Overseas Ministries and Week of Compassion monies, the Disciples had more than $6 million in overseas involvement in 1985. Week of Compassion, a February offering similar to the One Great Hour of Sharing in other churches, is aimed at relief and development efforts and support of the ecumenical movement around the world. About a third of the grants from the fund go through the World Council of Churches aid channels and another third through the U.S. National Council of Churches (Church World Service). A significant portion of the remainder is held for emergency use in the disasters that occur on an average of every 15 days. By the mid-1980s contributions to Week of Compassion had grown to nearly $2.5 million annually.

* * *

"Stories of . . . exemplary individuals are an important part of the tradition that is so central to a community of memory."

On the porch of his ranch house in south central Africa, R. S. GARFIELD TODD was looking out across the rolling, scrub-covered plains. He was over six feet tall, with dark wavy hair

161

whitening on the sides, a handsome, rugged complexion. He spoke rapidly, a biographer said he poured forth 200 words a minute. Though white, he was a happy citizen of the new black-ruled Zimbabwe. He had played a role in bringing it about. He was a senator in the new government. Independence had come April 18, 1980. Robert Mugabe, who had once been a teacher in the mission school administered by Todd, was the prime minister.

Twenty two years earlier Todd himself had been the prime minister of what then was called Southern Rhodesia. He lost the job because his fellow whites were horrified over his determination to bring blacks into rightful power. The blacks dated the ouster of Garfield Todd from his party's leadership as the beginning of the revolution. There no longer was a chance of a political solution.

Todd was 72 years old now. The revolution had brought death to 6,000 people in its last seven years. As a Christian, he was pained by the violence. "But I can't be completely pacifist," he had said. "I have seen the patience of the people and how they have suffered. I believe in being a peacemaker. But there has to be some basis on which to establish peace. And that basis is justice."

Todd and his wife came to Southern Rhodesia as Disciples of Christ missionaries from New Zealand. That was in 1934. They were in charge of the Dadaya Mission School near Shabani. Many of their students become leaders of the revolution. And as the revolution neared its end, Todd had gone to London as advisor to the black leaders in the peace talks.

Under the Ian Smith regime in Rhodesia, Todd spent five weeks in solitary confinement, five years under house arrest. The ranch where he now stood had been his prison for those five years. Eight hundred paces from his front door was his travel limitation. A stranger stood at the edge of his property every day, watching. He wasn't allowed to have visitors, write letters, or telephone.

Things had changed rapidly in Africa since 1960. Following World War II there were only four independent nations on the continent, now suddenly in 1960 there were 17 new ones joining the six created in the 1950s as colonialism collapsed with a thud. Northern Rhodesia became Zambia in 1964 but the British Crown Colony of Southern Rhodesia hung on. Blacks outnumbered whites 22 to 1 but there appeared to be as little hope for black rule in Southern Rhodesia (changed to Rhodesia when Zambia was born) as there was in neighboring South Africa. Ian Smith, representing the white ranchers and factory owners who ruled, was the Prime Minister. Britain was not resisting independence for Southern Rhodesia as much as it was delaying it until there could be some assurance of black participation in government.

Todd had had his own fling in the desert-rust-colored Parliament building across from the palm-shaded Cecil Square in Salisbury. When he and his wife arrived in in 1934, they bought the ranch above the Ngezi River. Dadaya mission school and Shabani were 200 miles southwest of Salisbury (now Harare). For a time, one of principal Todd's teachers was Mugabe, who thought Todd a bit autocratic in his operation.

From his teaching position, Todd took an interest in politics. In 1946, he was elected to the Southern Rhodesia parliament. Seven years later he had gained the leadership of the United Rhodesia Party which in turn gained the leadership of the country, making Todd Prime Minister. Once inside the one story, ranch-style prime minister's home with the circular drive near downtown Salisbury, Todd began talking eventual black rule. And that did not sit well with Rhodesian whites. After five years—in 1958—four right wing cabinet members resigned over his liberal policies, and Todd was out. Todd says flatly, "I was kicked out."

In 1960, he was vowing to stay out of politics. Not so. A year after he said it, he would be organizing a New Africa Party aimed at abolishing racial barriers. As racial difficulties mounted, Prime Minister Ian Smith declared unilateral independence from Britain in 1965, fearing that the British would push controlling whites into some accommodation with blacks. Todd immediately was restricted to his ranch by the government. He was under house arrest for a year. In 1972, as Britain and Rhodesia worked on independence proposals while black guerrillas stepped up their war against white rule, Todd and his daughter Judith protested the proposals and were arrested at the ranch, five carloads of armed officers descending on them and confiscating 10,000 documents, mostly related to the rancher's service in the Prime Minister's post. For five weeks Todd would be locked in solitary confinement, to be followed by a second house arrest—this one of four years duration. Then, apparently because of world pressure initiated by his daughter Judith, then living in London, Todd was

163

freed from house arrest. Within a few months he was in Geneva with his friend, Matabele leader Joshua Nkomo, helping the black nationalists in their negotiations with Britain and the Smith government about Rhodesia's future.

In the bloody revolutionary days before independence in 1980 Todd would maintain his support of blacks and their drive to self-determination. He would staunchly defend World Council of Churches anti-racism grants to the black liberation organizations. He advocated economic intervention by the West, but not military.

In January 1986, in London, Reginald Stephen Garfield Todd was knighted by Queen Elizabeth. Then Sir Garfield went back to the Zimbabwe that he loved, retiring to his ranch with the intent of writing memoirs. A black city councilman in the town of Kwe Kwe in the new Zimbabwe appreciatively spoke of the missionary-rancher-politician: "Garfield. He's one of us!"

12

Ecumenism:
Hallmark of Disciples Identity

1982—*Falkland Islands war* (April 2-June 15) . . . NEW82 draws 1,160 to Kansas City (May 10-12) . . . *Equal Rights Amendment fails* (June 30) . . . National Convocation elects lst woman president (Aug. 7) . . . *Palestinian camp massacres* (Sept. 15) . . . *Space shuttle 1st trip successful* (Nov. 16) . . . *First artificial heart transplant* (Dec. 2) . . . Disciples/Roman Catholics renew talks.

1983—Teegarden proposes nuclear ethics panel (Feb. 1) . . . *Weirton Steel bought by employees* (March 13) . . . *OPEC cuts oil prices* (March 14) . . . *Sally Ride 1st U.S. woman in space* (June 18) . . . World Council Assembly, Vancouver (July 24-Aug. 10) . . . *USSR downs Korean airliner* (Aug. 30) . . . Church Extension celebrates 100th birthday (Sept. 26) . . . San Antonio Assembly seeks end to Central America military aid (Sept. 23-28).

Newsweek magazine called it the greatest Christian breakthrough since the Reformation. The World Council of Churches called it a "theological convergence." Some ecumenists called it nothing short of a miracle. Over a period of nearly half a century the groundwork had been laid. Now the fruits were visible. Sponsored by the World Council, theologians representing a large bloc of the world's Christians—including Roman Catholics and some fundamentalist groups—had developed a convergence on matters of baptism, the Lord's Supper and the ministry—issues which have divided the Christian family for centuries. What "convergence" meant was that key theologians of the various bodies believed they had reached a common understanding. What it did not mean was that churches had taken official action on it.

The basis of the convergence was a growing understanding among the followers of Jesus that their Lord would have been tolerant of many approaches. Contrary to popular belief, unity did not mean uniformity; in fact, diversity was to be applauded, even cultivated. Openness to the various traditions was the rule.

165

That was a new gift of God's grace. It sounded almost like the Disciples' favorite platitude of the nineteenth century: "In essentials unity, in opinions liberty, in all things charity (or love)." The changes that were taking place in the ecumenical movement were a delight to most Disciples. Their history of Christian unity as the "polar star" upon which they fixed their course was tainted by their own record of two divisions and no unions since the 1832 event that made them a definable movement.

The World Council at Vancouver

More than 100 Disciples of Christ were in Vancouver, British Columbia, in July-August 1983, or just across the border at a satellite event in Bellingham, Washington, for the General Assembly of the World Council of Churches. Underneath a great, striped tent on the campus of the University of British Columbia, the fruits of the theological convergence were shared. The Assembly celebrated "Jesus, the Life of the World" and at the opening worship the symbols of life were brought forward, including a baby which a Zimbabwean woman put into the outstretched arms of the smiling general secretary, Philip Potter. The woman was a part of the Disciples of Christ community in Zimbabwe.

The "Lima Liturgy," named for the Peruvian city where the convergence finally was reached, was used for the first time by the World Council in worship. The Archbishop of Canterbury celebrated the Lord's Supper while flanked by pastors from a number of traditions. The Orthodox took part in the worship but still were unable to participate in the Lord's Supper.

Disciples ecumenical leaders responded positively to the Baptism, Eucharist and Ministry document. Few Disciples were aware how much of the document's drafting was done by young Disciples theologians loaned to the staff of the World Council of Churches in Geneva, Switzerland. It was part of the Disciples' commitment to the wholeness of the church to provide a staff member to the Council's faith and order commission, the body that deals with theological issues—particularly those that relate to Christian unity and to the organization of the church. Robert K. Welsh, vice-president of the Council on Christian Unity; Stephen V. Cranford, Mid-America regional minister; and Michael K. Kinnamon, professor at Christian Theological Seminary, each served in the staff position during a part of the drafting of the theological convergence on Baptism, Eucharist and Ministry (BEM).

The Disciples Theology Commission, in its response to the convergence document, said that Disciples could live with the principles enunciated—even though there was real question as to whether the constituency would be as open as the ecumenists on the issue of infant baptism. The commission made the point that Disciples universally agreed that someone who was baptized was baptized into the whole church and not just one particular arm or congregation of it.

Nor did Disciples believe in rebaptism. They considered baptism the biblical symbol of entry into the fellowship of the church. Therefore they would be open to diversity in the practice of it, the commission believed. In fact, Disciples had voted in 1975 in General Assembly for "mutual recognition of members" among the Consultation on Church Union denominations, promising to work toward removing any barriers to that mutual recognition.

Perhaps the amount of water in baptizing really wouldn't make too much of an issue for Disciples, though immersion certainly is a dramatic and authentic symbol, one that beautifully captures burial and resurrection with Jesus. But baptizing infants— that was a tougher question. Baptism into the church was for persons old enough to make a conscious decision about the meaning of the step. In believer's baptism by immersion Disciples emphasized the human response to God's grace. Christians who baptized infants, on the other hand, were emphasizing God's unearned grace and the incorporation of the child into the fellowship of God's care.

Bishops, Presbyters, Deacons

The ministry was another element of the BEM that Disciples examined closely. The World Council of Churches document and the Consultation on Church Union consensus both acknowledged three ministerial offices: bishops, presbyters and deacons. Those were all biblical terms. Disciples would have difficulty with bishops who wielded authority over people's lives and, in fact, many Disciples still held that stereotype of the episcopal function. The understanding that presbyters (pastors) or elders normally would be the only persons who presided at the Lord's Supper

167

would disturb some, not others. The idea that deacons would be ordained would be a little strange in light of the Disciples' understanding of the meaning of diaconate.

Disciples came to this point from a rekindled ecumenical spirit dating to the turn of the century. In the latter half of the nineteenth century Disciples lost some of their original Christian unity spirit in the competition for followers and the building of mission. Growth and expansion were a part of the Disciples philosophy of the period just as it was that of the United States. Some 30 Disciples were involved in the 1905 meeting that initiated the Federal Council of Churches.

It was 1910 when the modern ecumenical movement got its start—dating from an International Missionary Conference in Edinburgh, Scotland. Disciples were there, but not prominently. Baltimore pastor Peter Ainslie set in motion that year the organization that came to be the Disciples Council on Christian Unity. Disciples were present in the beginnings of the ecumenical missionary, faith and order, life and work, relief and refugee, Sunday School and other associations which were the ingredients for the World Council of Churches in 1948. In fact, wherever some interchurch arrangement was going on, it was a good bet that Disciples were somewhere in the thick of it. The Disciples were organizers of the National Council of Churches in the United States in 1950, Roy G. Ross becoming its second general secretary.

The Catholics and Orthodox

Bernard Cardinal Law of Boston was a Mississippi diocesan newspaper editor when Disciples and the Roman Catholics began two-way theological talks in 1966, entering through a door opened by Pope John XXIII's Vatican II, just concluded the year before. Father Law was named to the dialogue team. He didn't know much about these Disciples of Christ. So prior to the first meeting at Christian Theological Seminary in Indianapolis he did some reading. When he arrived at the meeting he had an insightful and tongue-in-cheek comment to make: "You know, Disciples and Catholics have much more in common than I first would have imagined. We are both churches in which the Mass (Lord's Supper) is central to every worship. The difference is that we make it so sacred it is not always available; you make it so available it surely could not always be sacred!"

The bilateral conversations with the Roman Catholics obviously had a far different objective than the COCU or United Church of Christ talks. These were a sharing of theological views with better understanding in mind. The bilaterals continued annually through the Searching Years. In the mid-1970s, one series of the talks resulted in the Catholic participants getting a warning and some guidelines from Rome about public statements. The Disciples and Catholics concluded discussions of the Lord's Supper in a St. Louis session with a statement indicating there seemed to be no theological barrier to intercommunion between the two bodies. That was a little much for the Catholic hierarchy. From that moment on a bishop headed the Catholic delegation.

In the 1980s the dialogues with the Roman Catholics were upgraded to an international basis, with Disciples and Catholics from other countries involved as well as the United States and Canada. The significance of this was that Roman Catholics worldwide were involved in only five similar conversations with other religious groups.

A new and particularly exciting bilateral conversation with the Russian Orthodox Church began in 1987, with a visit of Disciples participants to the Soviet Union. The visit presumably will be returned in 1989. That conversation offered possibilities of discussions about the role of the church in preventing nuclear war between churches whose members represent the social fabric of the opposing superpowers. The Disciples made an important witness to the Russians. Nancy Heimer, leader development director for the Disciples Department of Church Women, became the first woman to deliver a theological paper at the Russian Orthodox seminaries in both Leningrad and Odessa.

Language barriers produced a major but amusing error in the Soviet Union. General Minister and President John Humbert did not arrive on the scheduled flight and the Russian Orthodox priest who was to drive him 75 miles to the seminary picked up the wrong man! When the two, who couldn't communicate, arrived at the seminary, it was discovered that the passenger was a Swedish seaman with a name sounding similar to that of Humbert. The poor seaman, expecting a night on the town and pleased at the Russian hospitality, found himself instead in an isolated seminary miles from his destination and confronting an embarrassed priest.

The experience of the Consultation on Church Union laid groundwork for the Disciples and the United Church of Christ to establish an ecumenical partnership in 1985. It may also have changed the course of church union for history. Once COCU had established principles of faith, worship, ministry and sacraments that the delegates themselves could abide, they began to translate that into a Plan of Union which was unveiled in 1970. Difficulties arose not so much on matters of faith, worship, ministry and sacraments, but on the structure which the COCU delegates naively outlined in their document. The result was a pullback and a start on something new to church union anywhere in the world. The new idea was to permit union to grow from the ground up and to consider it as a process rather than a plan.

"Living our way to union," as the process ecumenism was called, injected a new set of intentions: it involved a much slower pace, offered less control to church bureaucrats, and looked toward an indefinable form. It also failed to excite news media. Its slowness might allow the timetable to be God's. Its lack of control at the top might permit the broad base of membership to help shape the outcome. Its openness to form might give the Holy Spirit the opportunity to lead to something new.

A couple of unique models emerged, though with modest success. One was called the "generating community," which was a grouping of local churches of the COCU denominations in a given area who simply agreed to work together at whatever level they were able, reporting the results to the COCU leadership. Another was "Interim Eucharist Fellowships," groups of churches prepared to celebrate jointly the Lord's Supper on a regular basis. Church union efforts long had made clear that union did not imply uniformity, in fact, was just the antithesis of it. The ultimate union would embrace a great deal of diversity and the process approach to union would help discover how to live with diversity and would open the opportunity for new forms and flexibility to develop naturally.

COCU identified some of the factors other than faith, theology and structure that serve as barriers to union. Those factors included racism, sexism, institutionalism and congregational exclusivism. COCU became the one forum in the United States continuing to deal with the toughest racism questions. With three of the nine participating churches in COCU being the historic black Methodist bodies and with union talks by necessity dealing with basic power sharing questions, COCU could not avoid some of the questions that other ecumenical bodies could submerge in good works.

In 1975, United Church of Christ president Robert Moss and Disciples general minister and president Kenneth Teegarden, on cue from the ecumenists in their ranks, jointly proposed a resumption of the union talks that had been suspended nearly a decade earlier between the two churches. The move was neither a challenge to COCU nor an expression of displeasure about its failure to come up with a suitable union plan. The UCCs and the Disciples might simply be able to model the union approach for COCU on a smaller scale. The principles of living toward union would be a logical way to go for churches as much alike as Disciples and UCCs.

In 1977, the Disciples and UCCs initiated conversation to test the waters about pursuing relations. That conversation period lasted two years. Then six years (1979-1985) went into study of (1) baptism and the Lord's Supper, (2) mission, and (3) ministry. At the end of that time the Disciples and UCCs covenanted between them for the beginning of an "ecumenical partnership," not knowing precisely where it would lead or how long it would take, though being quite certain God was calling the two churches to be in pursuit of the union ideal.

In the mid-1970s, British Disciples came up with the idea of a body officially representing the national churches of Disciples around the world to support ecumenical initiatives, develop common ecumenical strategies and provide a forum for concerns. The World Convention of Churches of Christ, which has existed since immediately after World War II, would not suffice as the vehicle. First of all, it maintained ties to all three branches of the Stone-Campbell movement, two of them—the Churches of Christ and the Independent Christian Churches—maintaining no relationships with the councils of churches or other mainline ecumenical elements. Also, the World Convention consisted of individuals from Campbell-Stone movement churches around the world, not representatives of the national church bodies.

The new body was called the Disciples Ecumenical Consultative Council and it held its first assembly in Kingston, Jamaica, in 1979. Among the guest speakers were Emilio Castro, later to become the general secretary of the World Council of Churches, and Jamaican Prime Minister Michael Manley. Due to fund limitations it has met in the United States in connection with General Assemblies of the North American Disciples since. It has played major roles in Disciples strategy for the World Council of Churches Assembly in Vancouver, British Columbia, in 1983 and in overseeing the Disciples-Roman Catholic dialogue.

One of the most extensive involvements in the ecumenical arena by Disciples was in the Christian education area. Joint Educational Development was a consortium of some 14 denominations, moving in and out as partners, depending on the projects. Disciples became a part of it in 1969. JED considered itself not an organization but a "covenantal relationship among persons of a number of denominations to work together on tasks that are important for church education." In a tested and updated statement in 1986 the JED denominations asserted: "We believe that as we work together we express the unity of the church, proclaim the gospel, and enhance our denominational ministries as well as contribute to the educational ministry of the whole church."

Even the Disciples' Christian Life Curriculum, which was the first new set of Christian education resources produced during the quarter century of the Searching Years, had its origins in planning of 18 denominations in 1962. It came into use in 1968. In the fall of 1970, a survey of 964 congregations showed 70 percent with a "very positive response" to the curriculum, but nearly 10 percent calling it "wholly unusable." The CLC continued in wide use until the next phase of curriculum began to unfold in 1976. That was the Christian Education: Shared Approaches curriculum. Its intent was to provide resources in four different approaches—ranging from pure Bible study to Christian involvement in the world—to help reach those who had been dissatisfied with curriculum in the past.

In mid-1976, as a part of an emphasis on renewing the congregation's educational ministry, Edu-Care came into being. It was a Disciples effort to train local leaders in the various aspects of the congregation's ministry and it was designed with workshops at the general, regional and congregational levels. Resources were ecumenically produced. Gradually other denominations began to participate in the training itself until by 1985 it was broadly ecumenical in character. In the first four years of Edu-

Care, 17,704 lay leaders had been trained along with 1,399 ministers. They came from 2,741 congregations.

One of the unique actions taken by Disciples in the mid-1980s in the ecumenical arena was to amend the *Design for the Christian Church (Disciples of Christ)* to allow for the election of four full voting members to the General Board from other denominations. It was the first time that any church had elected ecumenical representatives as full voting members of its board. The four persons—representing the United Church of Christ, Presbyterian Church in the USA, United Church of Canada, and Christian Methodist Episcopal Church—took their places at the Disciples' General Board in 1986 after election by the General Assembly in 1985.

If Disciples were concerned that the new board members might be timid about discussing and voting on internal Disciples matters, they underestimated both the people elected and the seriousness with which they took their responsibility! In that first General Board meeting in the summer of 1986, the United Church of Canada member took a strong social action position on one issue against the official recommendation. On another matter, the Presbyterian member freely entered into debate on the processes for calling a new General Minister and President, arguing that it was a mistake to insist on ordination as a qualification for the office. Both lost their points—Disciples treating them just as they would other board members!

* * *

"Stories of . . . exemplary individuals are an important part of the tradition that is so central to a community of memory."

It was her most exciting ecumenical moment but there were a couple of glitches. She stood next to the Archbishop of Canterbury, preparing to process into the sanctuary where she would read scripture and he would speak. He addressed her kindly. "You're going to sing, right?" "No, I'm reading scripture." Whoops. The archbishop had served with women on either side of him at the Holy Communion of the World Council of Churches Assembly in Vancouver in 1983 but stereotypes die hard, even for the distinguished clerical leader of Anglicans and

Episcopalians the world over. Then came another, like unto the first. A young man, seeing her standing there at the entrance to the sanctuary in her dress suit—she looked like a fashion model, which she was—concluded she was an impediment to the about-to-begin processional, and he offered her a seat. "I am IN the processional," she replied.

For NANCY V. STALCUP of Dallas, Texas, a laywoman and homemaker who frequently found herself the lone layperson and lone female in ecumenical settings, the incident was more amusing than aggravating. She did not permit it to detract from the exciting experience of sharing the leading of worship with persons of renown. She had been in precedent-setting positions on the Christian unity front before. On that day at Yale University for the Peter Ainslie Christian Unity Lectures, she was impressed but not overwhelmed—close-up she had seen the trembling hands of a male clergy colleague and she knew she was handling it better than he was.

"The thing about unity is that it is the most exciting part of the church," she said. "We all have different gifts. We have so much to give, whether we are Orthodox, or whatever. Unity gives us the opportunity to share the best of each. It is only for our asking and our looking for it. We must be expectant if unity is to come. We must ask for it and want it."

With that comment, Nancy Stalcup was echoing what many Disciples would acknowledge as both the special task and the special style of the Disciples of Christ. Yet few homemakers and mothers would have the opportunities she had for leadership in the task. And few would have had to make the switch she made to adopt the style. Nancy and her husband Joe were members of the Churches of Christ before they switched over to the Disciples in 1960. The Churches of Christ have a kinship to Disciples in that they came out of the same Campbell-Stone movement. But, far from being the United Church of Christ, the ecumenical dialogue partner of the Disciples of Christ, the Churches of Christ had an orientation more narrow and exclusive.

Though she and Joe were members of a Churches of Christ congregation that was not as conservative as others, Nancy Stalcup was bothered by "exclusiveness" in matters of faith. She had to have room to experience other Christians, grow in her understanding of mission and witness to the world, celebrate the diversity of the church. Also, she believed that Christians needed to "grow up" when it came to attitudes toward persons in foreign places, particularly those countries branded enemies by her own. While she loved her own country she cared about people who hurt, wherever they came from. At the same time, she appreciated the urgency of the Churches of Christ in telling the Good News. The Good News of Jesus Christ does pack an urgency, she believed.

Stalcup was 25 years into her married life, had raised three daughters and had a side career as a fashion model before she finally was free to accept her opportunities for leadership in the unity field: member of the Commission on Christian Unity for the Texas Conference of Churches (statewide, including Roman Catholic participation); co-chair with Joe of the Faith and Order Conference of the Texas Conference of Churches; vice-president of the Greater Dallas Community of Churches; a Community of Churches officer during the Dallas celebration of the World Council of Churches' Lima Liturgy; member of the board of directors of the Disciples of Christ Council on Christian Unity, chairperson of the Council on Christian Unity; member of the Disciples' first bilateral dialogue with the Russian Orthodox Church.

With her leadership credentials it should hardly surprise anyone that Nancy Stalcup was born in a log cabin. True. The place was northeast Texas—Hopkins County, some 80 miles from Dallas—in the depression years but just north of the nation's richest oilfield. Her father did some wildcatting but moved his family to Dallas in 1945, when Nancy was 11, so he could work in a defense plant. She was the baby of six children. At 17 she married 19-year-old Joe Stalcup who was destined to be a teacher, lawyer and a minister. By the time she was 22 she had three children. She attended Eastfield College and Southern Methodist University in Dallas. Joe started law school in 1956 and Nancy began modeling clothes for fashion markets, shows and catalogs. Except for the modeling, she spent the next several years "just being a mother," but that included being a Camp Fire leader and Parent Teacher Association board member.

"I don't know when we were not involved in the church," she recalled. "I've always been teaching Sunday School, working with children." Though her mother had a background in the Methodist and Baptist churches, her father had strong ties with the Churches of Christ which Nancy attended from early childhood. She was baptized into the Churches of Christ and Joe was ordained by them in 1951. In 1960 their search for a less exclusive and less pietistic fellowship brought the Stalcups to East Dallas Christian Church. The pastor was W. A. Welsh. He had a great deal of influence in their lives, she says. She began her church leadership involvements there in Christian Women's Fellowship, which she termed a marvelous training ground. She became president of the East Dallas CWF. Then she was elected president of the Dallas area association of the CWF.

It was not until 1975—the youngest child then being 19—that Nancy began her new phase of leadership involvement with the church, largely an ecumenical involvement. Joe, a successful lawyer with his own firm, decided to go to seminary, which he did, and Nancy went with him, auditing the courses for no credit. Joe was ordained in 1978. She found the faith commitment she wanted to express at a gathering of the Texas Conference of Churches to which she accompanied her husband. She got involved personally with the Texas Conference in its faith and order efforts, followed by election to the offices mentioned. Nancy and Joe have backed up their commitments to the Disciples of Christ and the wider church with large financial gifts. But they prefer that involvement to be a quiet one.

She was elected to the Disciples Council on Christian Unity board in 1978 and has been a decision-maker for Disciples about the church's ecumenical involvements ever since. In 1986 she became chairperson of the Council's board. In her capacity with the Council she took part in the first of the Disciples' dialogues with the Russian Orthodox Church in April 1987. That conference took place in the Soviet Union. Her earlier expressed feeling for all of humanity was fortified in the conversations with the Russian Orthodox. Stalcup was deeply moved with the thousand years of history of the Orthodox Church compared with the less than 200 years of the Disciples.

The Russians have a great tradition to share, one in which they use all five senses in worship. She observed high devotion in the use of chanting, robes, incense, icons, and celebration of Holy Communion. In fact, both churches have gifts that would benefit the other, if not the world, in terms of modeling peace between citizens of "enemy" nations.

13

The Search Continues

1984—*Breakup of AT&T* (Jan. 1) . . . *Congress condemns Nicaragua harbor mining* (April 10) . . . Teegarden offers identity statement at General Board (June 23) . . . World Convention held at Kingston, Jamaica (July 18-22) . . . *Los Angeles Olympics open* (July 28) . . . *Indira Gandhi assassinated* (Oct. 31) . . . *Sandinistas win election* (Nov. 4) . . . *Chemical leak at Bhopal, India, kills 2,000* (Dec. 3) . . . COCU adopts theological consensus (Dec. 3).

1985—Disciples send $108,000 to Ethiopia relief (Jan. 4) . . . *Mandela rejects South Africa freedom offer* (Feb. 10) . . . *Bangladesh cyclone kills 40,000* (May 25) . . . *Israelis pull out of Lebanon* (June 10) . . . Disciples' Sang Jung Park heads Christian Conference of Asia (July 2) . . . *Greenpeace ship sunk in New Zealand* (July 10) . . . Ecumenical Partnership with United Church of Christ okayed (Aug. 3) . . . Humbert elected general minister (Aug. 3) . . . *Achille Lauro highjacked* (Oct. 7) . . . *Harare Declaration urges economic sanctions against South Africa* (Dec. 5-7).

Early in 1984, Kenneth Teegarden turned to the used IBM Selectric typewriter on the stand at the left of his desk and began composing a statement. He had been reading the research that said the Disciples of Christ had virtually no identity among the general public, that they had little knowledge of their own heritage, and that they were defensive about their non-image. He would compose a "marketing" statement. You had to know who you were before you could tell other people. The self-description needed to be short and punchy. Texas Christian University had one of 17 words. All of the university's communication strategy was built around it. When he finished pecking away and had penciled a few changes, he leaned back in his chair and looked at it. Sixty-eight words. He tested it around the office.

That summer he tried it on the General Board. There was lots of discussion—mostly about things people thought absolutely had to be in a statement describing the Disciples. He offered through the General Board Report an opportunity for all congregations to respond. Feedback offered more suggestions—mostly about things people thought absolutely had to be included. He listened to all of the comments and rewrote it. Now it had an even hundred words.

> The Christian Church (Disciples of Christ) is a community of believers who through baptism into Jesus Christ are bound by covenant to God and one another. Disciples draw their inspiration from Scripture and the Holy Spirit, celebrating around the Lord's Table the life, death, resurrection and continuing presence of Christ. They proclaim the Good News of salvation and claim as their particular mission the quest for Christian unity. While stressing freedom and diversity under God, they believe unity and mission are inseparable. They witness and serve among the whole human family in the interest of peace, justice, mercy and kindness.

As Disciples wandered through the second decade of their new structure, they sought through professional research to discover their identity as a people. They were told: they are virtually unknown to the general public (George Gallup reported that one-third of the population says they know Disciples but even that third is largely confused). They have a low self-image which hampers evangelism (media research in Alabama indicated the greatest value of TV ads and billboards was in encouraging Disciples to talk about their church with others). They have a profile that depicts them as largely older female lay persons and younger male ministers. The Division of Homeland Ministries' 1986 questioning of 12,165 Disciples showed: Ministers are 97 percent male and 60 percent under age 50; laity is 64 percent female and 65 percent over 50. They see as the top priorities for the church: (1) Christian education, (2) spiritual growth, and (3) strengthening families, according to the DHM study. They see as the Disciples' strongest selling points their "acceptance" of all kinds of people, their diversity and their freedom, according to Office of Communication focus group research in Dallas and in Hannibal, Missouri.

An Identity as Peacemakers

While Disciples were being thus advised as to who they were, Disciples were deciding for themselves that in the 1980s they would be peacemakers. Disciples had declined in General Assembly to declare themselves a "peace church"—not because they didn't want to be, but because it wasn't a fact; they had no history to claim such a thing and no theology that could insist on a common mind about it. But they came about as close as they could to being of one mind on peace as their agenda for the 1980s.

"Peace with Justice" became the denominational priority in 1981, continuing through mid-decade. In response to the peace with justice priority, Kenneth Teegarden, with the approval of the Administrative Committee, appointed a blue ribbon Panel on Christian Ethics in a Nuclear Age, which after a two-year study produced the volume *Seeking God's Peace in a Nuclear Age*. It was another restructure first—the first major moral commentary on a public issue growing out of the new denominational priorities and processes.

Teegarden's Panel on Christian Ethics in a Nuclear Age put the identity question squarely: "Amid the sound and fury of all the new weapons and all the old angers every Christian heart is summoned to be a maker of peace. Although we are tempted to ignore the call to peacemaking, we do not have the option to refuse the challenge. Our faith demands that we respond as individuals and as a church with daring new vision and bold new ventures for the making of peace." The panel declared to Disciples that the arms race is unacceptable, that threatening mass annihilation cannot be endured, that the idea of a limited nuclear war is dangerous, that the United States should join the Soviet Union in a pledge to no first nuclear strike, that economic dependence on the war industry must be reversed, that Christians need to be tolerant of each other's views on the matter, and finally that "no use of nuclear arms can meet the requirements of a just war." Affirmed the panel: "We therefore advocate nuclear pacifism."

Three major issues confronted the Disciples as the restructure era ended.

Issue: Funding and Priorities

The General Board's task force on renewal and structural reform set in motion in 1987 a study intended to get to the root of the funding questions that have bedeviled Disciples before restructure and since. How does the church fund its mission? How does it fund priorities? What is the best way to allocate the resources? How does the church shift its resources? How does it halt funding a particular program altogether?

Several times during the Search for Identity years Disciples struggled with the priorities question. The Commission on Finance—which allocates Basic Mission Finance dollars—frequently maintained that it is not within its competence or role to weigh one program against another. Its task is simply to hear the pleas of the organizations of the church and respond from available resources. But how do you do that without either making some judgment as to which are the better programs or simply maintaining the percentage shares?

The General Board has no budget with which to fund priorities. When a priority is established, units, regions and institutions of the church must shift monies voluntarily if the priority is to be underwritten. Protocol insists that hard suggestions are taboo. And when an arm of the church is operating in a period of inflation that surpasses receipts, its concentration is on "maintaining" the work that its staff has been specifically called to do.

The allocations process is geared to prevent disruption, not permit flexibility. There is a 1 percent "adjustment fund" that is withheld from every organization's allocation. The adjustments allowed are for inequities and emergencies, not priorities. Frequently, when there were no valid emergencies or inequities, the fund—totaling in recent years some $160,000 a year—simply was returned to the overjoyed units from which it had been deducted.

While Disciples have systemitized their Basic Mission Finance handling well, there remain substantial difficulties in the development of special gifts, long-term funding and endowments. Development officers abound in various Disciples organizations as well as in the Christian Church Foundation. In recent years those officers have been meeting annually but much remains to remove the competitive factor from their work.

Issue: Roles of the Regional and General Church

With the regional share of the world outreach offerings having gone from 29 percent to 36 percent since the arrival of restructure, more than a million dollars a year now is being spent in regions that would have gone to general work under the old percentages. That inevitably is the source of tension between the two manifestations. The general units lament that there will be no end to the shift of monies to the regions since general units receive firm allocations, the regions only recommendations subject to negotiation.

The regions, in turn, argued that the responsibility is shifting their way, that the move is to decentralization, citing one of John Naisbitt's ten Megatrends of the 1980s. Some regions also maintained that monies given by congregations in a region ought to pass through the regional hands first, where regions extract a share and pass on the remainder. General unit people countered that that would violate the spirit of equal manifestations and emulate a pyramidal style of structure, which Disciples meticulously avoided.

Both could cite the whipsaw effect: As general unit resources dwindle, programs are dumped; as programs are dumped, regions have to develop their own, necessitating more resources; etc., etc., etc. The issue, of course, is more than money. What are the proper roles in ministry of regions and general units? Since the restructured church is comprised of equal manifestations, who decides what the region and general roles will be?

The question about roles crops up again in inquiries about the possibilities of a "fourth manifestation"—in addition to congregational, regional and general. Many large regions now have districts or areas to bring pastoral relationships closer to the congregations. Is the regional role more pastoral or administrative? Which should it be? Does it have anything to say about the general role? The need for a fourth manifestation?

Issue: Challenges to Programming

In the old days when a Disciple didn't think a program of ministry was working as it should, the dissatisfied soul simply gathered friends of a like mind and started a new one. Then she/he arranged for the church to support it. That's how the church came to have three major missionary societies which merged in 1920 into the United Christian Missionary Society. Restructure was intended to provide the authority that would prevent the rise of competitive programs and their linkage to the church. It also was intended to provide a means for the members at large to correct and redirect existing programs they feel are not adequately carrying out the mission.

Due to the denomination's 22-year membership decline considerable dissatisfaction was evident among Disciples in pulpits and pews over evangelism. The Division of Homeland Ministries' evangelism and membership department produced numerous programs during the quarter century (such as Growth for Witness, Adventures in Evangelism, Order of Andrew, Movin' Family) but the denominational membership reversals continued.

The National Evangelistic Association is listed in the *Design for the Christian Church (Disciples of Christ)* as one of the seven "other organizations" officially recognized by the church. Its principal function prior to 1977 was fellowship for persons with strong evangelistic interests; in fact it began in 1904 as an organization for professional evangelists. In 1968 its program consisted of a pre-International Convention meeting for preaching and inspiration.

Herbert J. Miller Jr. was a pastor in Hobbs, New Mexico, when restructure was voted. He became the regional minister of New Mexico and then a Southwest area minister when New Mexico and Texas merged in 1973. Energetic and entrepreneurial, Miller capitalized on the cry for effective evangelism among Disciples, traveling widely and conducting workshops on the subject, writing prolifically, researching and producing resources and strategies for church growth.

He and others involved in the National Evangelistic Association resolved in 1977 to build the NEA membership, undertake fund development for it, and engage it in evangelism programs. His periodical, *NET Results*, and his workshop leadership eventually attracted other denominations as well as Disciples. He initiated a biennial national evangelism workshop (NEW) in 1980 that grew in attendance to over 1,300 people.

Rather than have competitive evangelism programs, the Division of Homeland Ministries evangelism and membership department signed agreements with the NEA in which they exchanged board members, used Miller as a consultant jointly, and developed workshops and programs together. Six years after Miller had brought NEA into full-scale programming, the operation had grown too large for its eight-room suite in Lubbock, Texas, and Miller was able to arrange for a building that was NEA's own. The following year, May 8, 1984, Miller became NEA's first full time executive director.

While general unit executives objected to Miller's constant rhetoric about the decline of the church and the implication that he had the solution, real difficulty came when NEA began raising money directly from congregations in support of its burgeoning operations. NEA, not being an administrative unit of the Disciples of Christ and not a recipient of regular outreach funds, wasn't subject to the rules barring such direct solicitations. That brought church leadership to make inquiry of NEA as to its intentions relative to entry into the Church Finance Council processes. With rapid growth in funding from congregational sources and a church constituency eagerly seeking evangelism help, NEA displayed what appeared to be a reluctance.

The question for Disciples became one of determining who was running the church's evangelism program and whether it was the general administrative unit to which the task had been assigned. If in fact NEA was doing evangelism on behalf of the church should it not come under the same fund-raising disciplines as other program units who must share the church's outreach dollar? What recourse do Disciples have if they are not satisfied with the program they are receiving from authorized units? Can they effect a change or must they engage a new "agency," as in the pre-restructure days?

Working Well Despite All

The beauty is: that the funding system has worked as well as it has, that the regions and general units have worked together as well as they have, and that programs have been carried out as well as they have considering the voluntarism, natural protectiveness, mutuality, newness, structural looseness, individual wills and ambitions, the natural tendency to revert to the past, sniping from the outside and the budget strain. The reason that it has worked as well as it has is that there is a genuine desire among the bureaucrats involved to demonstrate the wholeness of the church. It is one of the fruits of restructure.

The collegiality among top leadership of the Christian Church (Disciples of Christ) was markedly different in 1985 than it was in 1968. Leaders, with few exceptions at the regional and general levels, want to play their role as a part of the whole church. Their abilities may fail them but they genuinely are open to the leading of the Holy Spirit.

The quarter century that began with the call for a Commission on Brotherhood Restructure ended with a call issued to John

O. Humbert to become the church's third General Minister and President. Teegarden, architect and shaper of restructure, retired from the chief executive position shortly after the 1985 Des Moines General Assembly. The choice of his successor underscored the emphasis on the pastoral. Humbert, an Ohioan, served eight years as Teegarden's deputy but he was first and foremost a local pastor. For 28 years he was the pastor of churches in Ohio, Kentucky and Maryland. He was the son and grandson of pastors in a family that numbered 14 ministers in seven generations going back to great-great-great grandfather James Foster, who came with the Campbells from Ireland and who presided when Alexander Campbell preached his ordination sermon near Washington, Pennsylvania.

Humbert set a high tone for his administration by appointing as his deputy the person who had been a strong second choice for his own position, Donald O. Manworren of Iowa, and then adding two women to the all-male General Cabinet (there had not been a woman on Cabinet since Jean Woolfolk retired in 1983). He picked up on the "peace with justice" priority only a few months into office by traveling to Geneva where along with Russian church leaders he prayed for success of the beginning arms control talks.

Despite the stirrings on behalf of evangelism among Disciples and the success of such programs as Church Advance Now (in developing 100 new congregations within the decade), the sociologists and the theologians don't give Disciples or any other "mainline" churches much hope of a turnaround in the membership slide—perhaps a leveling off. Sociologists Wade Clark Roof and William McKinney (the latter the nephew of the late executive of men's work among the Disciples) argued that with faith a highly individualized, private matter the churches that encourage freedom of choice (as Disciples do) come out the big losers. Roof and McKinney said in a 1985 study that mainline Protestantism "is shrinking and will continue to do so for the foreseeable future." Martin Marty wrote in 1985 that mainline Protestants will continue to lose ground to the fundamentalists because they do not have the "competitive potency" of the born-again or charismatic Christians. Further, they are not willing to fall back on the authority claims—"The Bible says"—that the fundamentalists do, nor are they willing to pass stringent judgment on people's fitness to be a part of their fellowship. The mainline church person cannot bring herself or himself to respond to the current American passion for "personal experience, authority in the face of relativism and chaos, and the pull toward institutions and movements that provide personal identity and social location," Marty wrote.

Nor is that likely to change. It would fly in the face of what Disciples see as their identity. A 1987 conference on the Disciples' identity was attended by more than 500 interested church leaders from all levels, including the more conservative and including all three of the persons who have served as General Minister and President. That Christian Theological Seminary, Indianapolis, conference concluded: "The Christian Church (Disciples of Christ) has a distinctive identity worth preserving. We have been a church characterized by attention to the biblical witness (and not any particular tradition about the Bible), by an orientation to reasonableness (that is, a willingness to use methods of human thought to understand the gospel), and by our commitment to the unity of the church (rooted in our aching sense that we are not the whole)." Grounded in all of these is the conviction that "our ways may not be God's ways and thus they must always be open to critique."

Those elements of the Disciples' identity enumerated by the conference are not what the Roofs, McKinneys and Martys say assures numerical success in religious faith. The growing groups insist on a particular tradition about the Bible. They proclaim an authority and interpretation that is not based upon reasonableness. Their witness is sectarian and competitive with other Christians, not rooted in unity and openness. And hardly are their affirmations open to critique. Yet, would Disciples want to change the key elements of their identity, their theology, to achieve worldly success?

The 1987 conference at Christian Theological Seminary in Indianapolis on the Disciples' identity and future was unwilling to concede evangelism to the fundamentalists and charismatics, however. The conference declared: "The common wisdom today is that a church cannot be ecumenical and evangelistic, that we will sacrifice one or the other. Wrong! Evangelism and ecumenism are related and shared aspects of the one faith and integral to who we are; to give up either of them is to give up our identity."

Newsweek magazine said in December, 1986 that mainline Protestants must accept the fact of minority status, that they no longer are the mainline. Marty says the mainliners have lost their privileged status and must now challenge from the outside. While Marty sees no return of mainline Protestants to the prominence they once held in religion he does believe they will survive and have a renewal of their own. "They are likely to serve a more modest but still important roll as advocates of sorts of tolerance in an increasingly tribal world." Further, the mainline Protestants "are even likely to clarify their own views of experience, authority, and identity, and to minister to those who seek what they offer while also acquiring a new status as dissenters." Roof and McKinney think likewise: "Despite the plight of the liberal Protestant mainline currently, the moderate Protestant faiths may recover a new middle ground. By virtue of their size and heritage, moderate to liberal groups are in a position and have the resources to forge a broadly-based synthesis of belief and culture." *Newsweek* says the former Protestant mainline may draw new vitality from its minority status.

Just as Disciples find themselves in a period in time which is really no period but an in-between, Roof and McKinney declare the present religious situation in North America as one with a left and a right and no center. The broadly-based synthesis of belief and culture that they talk about is going to come from Christians who are able to engage other groups, who can generate a social vision capable of broadly encompassing middle America, and who are deeply rooted in the life of the people. That is an identity not far from where Disciples have seen themselves.

Out of the quagmire of individualism, it is the Disciples' destiny to preach reconciliation. The Christian faith is in community—a covenant community. The world is a family, a family of God's children. The strength of the restructured church is that it models unity with diversity, freedom with responsibility. The strength of Disciples—perhaps not in the competition for numbers—is that their ways are ways of reasonableness, always open to critique.

No group of people is in any better position to claim the ministry of reconciliation as its priority. While the data may reflect that the church is aging, the younger theologians and leaders abound—the Michael Kinnamons, Nadia Lahutskys, Clark Gilpins, Rick Harrisons, Beverly Gaventas, Jim Dukes and Tony

Dunnavants, to name a few. To quote the first moderator of the restructured church, Ronald Osborn, for a final time: "We have a caliber of intellectual leadership far surpassing that available to the Panel of Scholars, a leadership of genuine distinction committed to the life of the church and significantly involved in its life."

* * *

"Stories of . . . exemplary individuals are an important part of the tradition that is so central to a community of memory."

As is often the case in the study of scripture, a previously unnoticed phrase fairly leaped out from a familiar passage. The story was Jesus' encounter with the woman at the well from John 4. But what struck the pastor as she was preparing her sermon were the words, "on his way (to Galilee) he had to go through Samaria." He had to go through Samaria. Samaria—that hated place populated by a mixed race of Hebrews and Assyrian captives forced into settling there. Most people went around Samaria, perhaps down the Jordan river valley. But Jesus had to go through Samaria.

REBECCA J. BUNTON thought how beautifully that dramatized the theme of Lent: Jesus believing there were certain things he had to do to keep his integrity. How often people put walls and barriers around folks with whom they don't want to deal. But Jesus couldn't do that. He had to go through Samaria. There are places into which Christians are called to go, Bunton thought, just to make the word credible. Jesus said, "You shall be my witnesses." Growing in Christ required going through, not around, the Samarias of this world.

When the pastor took the pulpit on that Lenten Sunday morning in New Palestine, Indiana, she felt deeply moved by the spirit. The sermon was one of her best. She knew it. Members of the congregation were struck by it. They told her so. It was simple, straightforward—a message that reached each person in a different way.

There are some encounters with people that would be easier left undone. But the spirit demands, for integrity's sake, a trip through Samaria. As a woman senior minister Becky Bunton could recall one of her own. It happened at the outset of her

187

ministry in New Palestine, a tiny bedroom community 20 miles southeast of Indianapolis. She called on an elderly couple. The man was brutally frank; he didn't believe in women in the pulpit. He didn't think he had a church anymore. "Can you preach?", he asked. But whatever the answer he didn't intend to come. "I was hurt when I left," the pastor recalled. "I cried a lot." The man didn't come to church. But Rev. Bunton continued to call on the couple at home, regularly, as if nothing had happened, and only they mattered. They developed a relationship, the couple returned to active church participation and just before the man died, he told the pastor he wanted her to have his automobile. She couldn't accept it, she felt, but the widow sold it and gave the proceeds to the church.

Becky Bunton had come to the New Palestine congregation in 1979. The congregation was a little less than average size for Disciples, about 200 members, 104 of them "participating." The median size for Disciples congregations is 138. In six years of her ministry the participation increased by 25 percent.

The New Palestine minister was born in December of 1943 in Wichita, Kansas. She grew up in a rural area, and went to a rural grade school. Her parents would like to have been farmers, but settled for a cow, a pig, a few chickens and an orchard. She had two older brothers and a younger sister but she remained shy. She was musically inclined, learning the piano when she was seven. She attended Friends University, a Quaker school. She maintains a sign on the shelf behind her desk at the church that is a reminder of the Quaker tradition, "Silence spoken here." She majored in elementary education and minored in music.

Her family, if not at home, was in the Fairview Christian Church. They handled the custodial work as well as other church tasks. She was the organist. She served as one of the counselors at a summer church camp where two Kansas pastors, Jim L. Beaumont and Roy L. Helms, asked her if she had thought about the ministry. She was searching for herself at the time, knowing only that she had to get out on her own; she had lived at home even while attending college. Her pastor, Carl Hall, was encouraging regarding the ministry.

One day in 1966 Alice Cobble, a Kansas missionary, spoke at the church on "For Such a Time as This," and Becky Bunton marched down the aisle and gave her life to full time Christian service. She never thought about anything other than the pastoral ministry, but most people she talked to could see women only as missionaries or religious education directors. Their comments felt like putdowns. They made her less than who she knew she could be.

Someone in the Fairview church had links to Christian Theological Seminary in Indianapolis, which was just beginning as the successor to the School of Religion at Butler University. She won a scholarship to the seminary as one of the handful of women outnumbered 25 to 1 by men. She was the only woman in many classes. Hers was the first class to complete its three years all in the new seminary campus adjacent to Butler. In many ways she still was searching for herself. Her theology classes helped her to identify how important God was to her.

During her seminary days she served as the minister of Christian education in Greenfield, Indiana, then as the minister of music and Christian education in Anderson, where she continued and was ordained after seminary completion. When she became the senior pastor in Stilesville, Indiana, in 1972 she was the only female senior pastor in the state. She realized she really didn't know how to counsel and in 1976 she entered clinical pastoral education training at the Indiana University medical school and later at Methodist Hospital in Indianapolis. From 1977 until 1979 she was resident chaplain at the Indiana University medical center.

It has not been easy being a woman in the pastorate. Despite her experience, people who meet her tend to address her as someone just out of school and facing the ministry. It's a new thing for many people. When she was in Stilesville she would find biblical quotes from Paul's letters to Timothy on her door—those quotes that refer to women not speaking in the church. People have to meet women pastors in the flesh to appreciate them, she says. While the number of women in senior pastorates and in training in the seminaries has multiplied at least four fold since when she began, she warns that any young woman entering the ministry still has a battle with tradition and prejudice and paternalism.

It remains difficult for men to come to her for counseling. But most counseling takes place informally in halls and parking lots and foyer anyway. That's okay by her. As long as it serves. She has a shy, serious demeanor that breaks into a broad smile as she talks. She feels she is sensitive, compassionate, accepting people where they are. "There is something that I can love about everybody."

And she is still searching, somewhat, for her full identity. She believes that might be a lifetime quest, for others as well as herself.